GRADE
2

CommonCore Language

M000302409

Table of Contents

Introduction

What Is the Common Core?

The Common Core State Standards are an initiative by states to set shared, consistent, and clear criteria for what students are expected to learn. This helps teachers and parents know what they need to do to help students. The standards are designed to be rigorous and pertinent to the real world. They reflect the knowledge and skills that young people need for success in college and careers.

If you teach in a state that has joined the Common Core State Standards Initiative, then you are required to incorporate these standards into your lesson plans. Students need targeted practice in order to meet grade-level standards and expectations, and thereby be promoted to the next grade.

What Does the Common Core Say About Language Standards?

In order for students to be college- and career-ready in language, they must gain control over many conventions of standard English grammar, usage, and mechanics as well as learn other ways to use language to convey meaning effectively.

Research shows that it is effective to use students' writing as a tool to integrate grammar practice. However, it is often hard to find a suitable context in which to teach such specific grade-level standards. Some students will need additional, explicit practice of certain skills. The mini-lessons and practice pages in this book will help them get the practice they need so they can apply the required skills during independent writing and on standardized assessments.

Students must also be proficient in vocabulary acquisition skills. This means being able to determine or clarify the meaning of grade-appropriate words. It also means being able to appreciate that words have nonliteral meanings, shades of meaning, and relationships to other words. These skills will enable students to read and comprehend rigorous informational texts and complex literary texts.

The Common Core State Standards state that the "inclusion of Language standards in their own strand should not be taken as an indication that skills related to conventions, effective language use, and vocabulary are unimportant to reading, writing, speaking, and listening; indeed, they are inseparable from such contexts."

Using This Book

Mini-Lessons and Practice Pages

Each grade-level volume in this series addresses all of the language standards for that grade. For each standard, three types of resources are provided that scaffold students using a gradual release model.

Based on your observations of students' language in writing and in collaborative conversations, choose mini-lessons that address their needs. The mini-lessons can be used during your literacy and writing block. Then use the practice pages to reinforce skills.

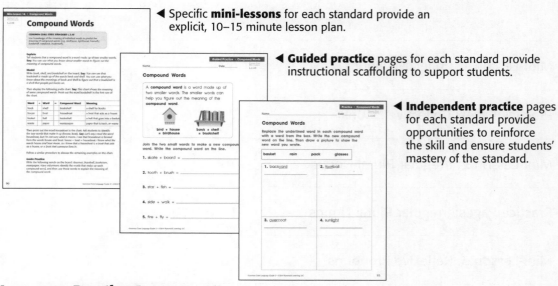

◀ Specific **mini-lessons** for each standard provide an explicit, 10–15 minute lesson plan.

◀ **Guided practice** pages for each standard provide instructional scaffolding to support students.

◀ **Independent practice** pages for each standard provide opportunities to reinforce the skill and ensure students' mastery of the standard.

Language Practice Assessments

Easy-to-use, flexible practice assessments for both Conventions and Vocabulary standards are provided in the last section of the book. The self-contained 2-page assessments cover skills in a reading passage format and have multiple-choice answers.

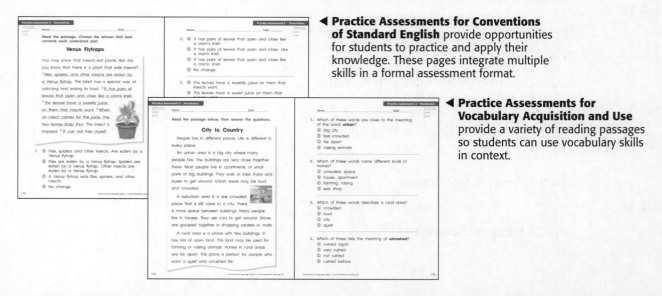

◀ **Practice Assessments for Conventions of Standard English** provide opportunities for students to practice and apply their knowledge. These pages integrate multiple skills in a formal assessment format.

◀ **Practice Assessments for Vocabulary Acquisition and Use** provide a variety of reading passages so students can use vocabulary skills in context.

Lesson Plan Teacher Worksheet

Conventions of Standard English and Knowledge of Language

The lessons in this section are organized in the same order as the Common Core Language Standards for conventions. Each mini-lesson provides specific, explicit instruction for a Language standard and is followed by multiple practice pages. Use the following chart to track the standards students have practiced. You may wish to revisit mini-lesson and practice pages a second time for spiral review.

Common Core State Standards	Mini-Lessons and Practice	Page	Complete (✓)	Review (✓)
L.2.1a	Mini-Lesson 1: Collective Nouns	6		
	Practice Pages: Collective Nouns	7		
L.2.1b	Mini-Lesson 2: Irregular Plural Nouns	10		
	Practice Pages: Irregular Plural Nouns	11		
L.2.1c	Mini-Lesson 3: Reflexive Pronouns	16		
	Practice Pages: Reflexive Pronouns	17		
L.2.1d	Mini-Lesson 4: Irregular Past Tense Verbs	20		
	Practice Pages: Irregular Past Tense Verbs	21		
L.2.1e	Mini-Lesson 5: Adjectives and Adverbs	26		
	Practice Pages: Adjectives and Adverbs	27		
L.2.1f	Mini-Lesson 6: Sentences	34		
	Practice Pages: Sentences	35		

Common Core State Standards	Mini-Lessons and Practice	Page	Complete (✓)	Review (✓)
L.2.2a	Mini-Lesson 7: Capitalization	48		
	Practice Pages: Capitalization	49		
L.2.2b	Mini-Lesson 8: Commas	56		
	Practice Pages: Commas	57		
L.2.2c	Mini-Lesson 9: Apostrophes	62		
	Practice Pages: Apostrophes	63		
L.2.2d	Mini-Lesson 10: Spelling Patterns	68		
	Practice Pages: Spelling Patterns	69		
L.2.2e	Mini-Lesson 11: Use Reference Materials for Spelling	72		
	Practice Pages: Use Reference Materials for Spelling	73		
L.2.3a	Mini-Lesson 12: Formal and Informal English	74		
	Practice Pages: Formal and Informal English	75		
	Answer Keys	126		

COMMON CORE
STATE STANDARD
L.2.1a

Collective Nouns

> **COMMON CORE STATE STANDARD L.2.1a**
> Use collective nouns (e.g., *group*).

Explain
Tell students that a collective noun names a group of people or things.

Say: *You know that a noun names a person, place, or thing. There is a special kind of noun that names a group of people, places, or things. The word* team *is a special noun like this because* team *names a group of people who play or work together.*

Ask: *Does the noun* group *name more than one person, place, or thing?* (yes) Continue with collective nouns *family* and *class*.

Model
Write this sentence on the board: *The team plays basketball*. Circle the collective noun *team*, and point out the singular verb. Explain that even though a team is a group, you use the singular form of a verb, the verb that matches one, with this kind of special noun.

Guide Practice
Write the sentences below on the board.

> *The family _____ going to the store.* (is)
> *The team_____ to school.* (Possible response: goes)
> *The group _____ lunch.* (Possible response: eats)
> *The class _____ on the bus.* (Possible response: gets)

Have a volunteer think of and use a verb to complete the first sentence, writing any verb that makes sense as long as it is singular. Then ask the student to read the completed sentence aloud.

Ask: *Did you write the singular form of the verb—the form for one—or the plural form—the form for more than one?* (singular; form for one) *Why?* (because *family* is a special kind of noun that names a group) Repeat the procedure with the remaining sentences.

Then tell students to use the nouns *family*, *team*, and *class* to write sentences about a game at school. Remind them to use the singular form of a verb with these words. Have them circle the collective nouns in their sentences.

COMMON CORE
STATE STANDARD
L.2.1a

Name_____ Date_____

Collective Nouns

A **collective noun** is a singular noun that refers to more than one person or thing.

a **group** of cats

a **class** of students

a **family** of four people

Draw a line to match each collective noun with the noun it names.

1. box of   **a.** birds

2. bunch of   **b.** trees

3. deck of   **c.** crayons

4. flock of   **d.** people

5. forest of   **e.** cards

6. crowd of   **f.** bananas

COMMON CORE
STATE STANDARD
L.2.1a

Name_____ Date_____

Collective Nouns

Circle the collective noun in each phrase. Then draw a picture to show it.

1. a long flight of stairs	**2.** a bouquet of yellow flowers
3. an old pair of shoes	**4.** a large crowd of people

Common Core Language Grade 2 • ©2014 Newmark Learning, LLC

COMMON CORE
STATE STANDARD
L.2.1a

Name_____ Date_____

Collective Nouns

> There are many **collective nouns** for animals.
>
> A group of bears is called a **sleuth**.
>
> A group of geese is called a **gaggle**.

Read each phrase. Underline the collective noun.

1. a den of snakes

2. a prickle of hedgehogs

3. a streak of tigers

4. a mob of emus

5. a charm of hummingbirds

6. a trip of sheep

7. a horde of hamsters

8. a knot of frogs

9. a pod of whales

10. a leap of leopards

Look at the collective nouns you underlined above. Find and circle each one in the puzzle.

L	E	A	P	D	E	N
C	M	T	R	I	P	L
H	X	Z	I	W	P	H
A	K	B	C	H	J	O
R	N	D	K	Y	M	R
M	O	B	L	P	O	D
S	T	R	E	A	K	E

COMMON CORE
STATE STANDARD
L.2.1b

Irregular Plural Nouns

> **COMMON CORE STATE STANDARD L.2.1b**
>
> Form and use frequently occurring irregular plural nouns (e.g., *feet, children, teeth, mice, fish*).

Explain

Remind students that a plural noun names more than one person, place, or thing. Explain that some plural nouns have special endings that students must learn and remember. Write the word *child* on the board.

Say: *You know the rules for adding* -s *or* -es *to form the plural of most nouns. But some nouns have special plural forms. They break the usual plural rules. You must remember the plural form of these nouns. For example, you don't form the plural of* child *by adding* -s *or* -es. *The plural form is* children. *Use the plural form* children *when there is more than one child doing something.*

Ask: *The noun* man *also has a special plural form. When you talk about more than one man, do you say* mans *or* men? (men)

Model

Write the following word pair on the board: *woman/women*. Read the words aloud, pointing out the irregular plural form. Model how to use the plural form in a sentence: *The women are at the park.* Have students repeat to make sure they get the pronunciation right. Repeat for *men* and *children*.

Guide Practice

Erase each plural form on the board. Ask students to say the plural form of each word. Provide prompts as necessary. When the list is complete, have students work with you to complete the following sentences with the singular and irregular plural form of *man, woman,* and *child*.

The _____ was happy. (man, woman, child)
The _____ were happy. (men, women, children)

Tell students to write the singular nouns *woman, child,* and *man* in their journals. Then have them write the plural form of each and use the plural noun in a sentence. Check that their sentences use the correct verb forms with each plural noun.

Name_____ Date_____

Form Irregular Plural Nouns

Irregular plural nouns are words that name more than one thing. They do not end in **-s** or **-es**. You must remember the plural forms of these nouns.

Draw a line to match each singular noun to its plural form.

1.

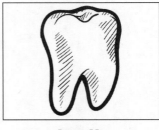

tooth

a.

fish

2.

fish

b.

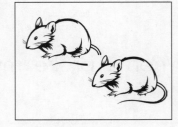

mice

3.

mouse

c.

teeth

COMMON CORE
STATE STANDARD
L.2.1b

Name_____ Date_____

Form Irregular Plural Nouns

Write the plural form of each underlined noun.

1. That <u>man</u> is my uncle.

_____

2. A <u>fish</u> swam to the top of the tank.

_____

3. Our class pet is a <u>mouse</u>.

_____

4. When I broke my <u>foot</u>, I got a cast for it.

_____

5. I lost my fourth <u>tooth</u>!

_____

6. One <u>child</u> is playing in the yard.

_____

Common Core Language Grade 2 • ©2014 Newmark Learning, LLC

Name_____ Date_____

COMMON CORE
STATE STANDARD
L.2.1b

Form Irregular Plural Nouns

Read each pair of sentences. Choose the plural form from the box to complete the second sentence.

geese	**people**	**sheep**	**women**

1. One goose flew away.

Two _____ flew away.

2. One sheep sat in the grass.

Three _____ sat in the grass.

3. That woman is my aunt.

Both of those _____ are my aunts.

4. That person is riding a bike.

Those _____ are riding bikes.

COMMON CORE
STATE STANDARD
L.2.1b

Name_____ Date_____

Use Irregular Plural Nouns

An **irregular plural noun** is a plural noun that does not end in **-s** or **-es**.

one sheep

two sheep

Write the correct form of the noun in ( ) to complete each sentence.

1. The two (mouse) ran in the hole. _____

2. I put shoes on my (foot). _____

3. The family has three (child). _____

4. Those (woman) are my aunts. _____

5. The group of (man) waited for the train.

_____

6. The two (person) looked up. _____

Common Core Language Grade 2 • ©2014 Newmark Learning, LLC

Name_____ Date_____

COMMON CORE
STATE STANDARD
L.2.1b

Use Irregular Plural Nouns

Write a sentence using the irregular plural noun for each word.

1. man

_____

_____

_____

2. person

_____

_____

_____

3. fish

_____

_____

_____

4. tooth

_____

_____

_____

COMMON CORE
STATE STANDARD
L.2.1c

Reflexive Pronouns

> **COMMON CORE STATE STANDARD L.2.1c**
> Use reflexive pronouns (e.g., *myself, ourselves*).

Explain

Tell students that a reflexive pronoun is a special pronoun that ends in *-self* or *-selves*. On the board, write: *I made myself lunch.*

Say: *You know that pronouns are words that take the place of other naming words. Some special kinds of pronouns end in* -self *or* -selves*. These are reflexive pronouns. They tell about the person or people doing the action in a sentence. In the sentence* I made myself lunch*, the pronoun* myself *tells about the word* I*. Draw an arrow from the subject* I *to the reflexive pronoun* myself.

Model

Write this sentence on the board: *We made ourselves lunch.* Draw an arrow from the word *ourselves* to the subject *we.* Explain that the word *ourselves* tells about the word *we,* or the people doing the action in this sentence.

Guide Practice

Have a student come forward to write this sentence as you dictate it: *We bought ourselves new clothes.* Have the student draw an arrow from the reflexive pronoun *ourselves* to the subject *We.*

Ask: *What does the arrow show?* (It shows that the word *ourselves* tells about the word *we.*) Repeat the routine for the pronoun *myself,* using the sentence: *I read the book by myself.*

Then write the sentences below on the board. Have volunteers write the pronouns *myself* or *ourselves* to complete each sentence, and then identify the word that each reflexive pronoun refers to.

> We made _____ comfortable. (ourselves, We)
> I poured _____ a glass of water. (myself, I)
> He made _____ laugh. (himself, He)
> She made _____ a sandwich. (herself, She)

For additional practice, tell students to write sentences using the reflexive pronouns *ourselves* and *myself* to tell about something they have done with other people, and then to tell about something they did on their own.

Name_____ Date_____

COMMON CORE
STATE STANDARD
L.2.1c

Reflexive Pronouns

> A **reflexive pronoun** is a special pronoun that ends in **-self** or **-selves**.
>
> I made **myself** lunch.
>
> He made **himself** lunch.
>
> We made **ourselves** lunch.

Read each sentence. Circle the reflexive pronoun.

1. She built a toy car all by herself.

2. They bought themselves a basketball.

3. I taught myself how to play piano.

4. Tim walked home from school by himself.

5. We clean our room ourselves.

COMMON CORE
STATE STANDARD
L.2.1c

Name_____ Date_____

Reflexive Pronouns

Write the correct reflexive pronoun to complete each sentence.

itself	myself	yourselves
ourselves	himself	

1. I saw _____ in the mirror.

2. Juan poured _____ a glass of water.

3. The dog tired _____ out running in the yard.

4. Please help _____ to snacks and drinks.

5. We kept _____ busy with a board game.

Common Core Language Grade 2 • ©2014 Newmark Learning, LLC

Name_____ Date_____

COMMON CORE
STATE STANDARD
L.2.1c

Reflexive Pronouns

Circle the reflexive pronoun in each sentence below. Then write a new sentence using that reflexive pronoun.

1. We painted the room ourselves.

_____

_____

2. I fell on the sidewalk and hurt myself.

_____

_____

3. Make yourselves comfortable.

_____

_____

COMMON CORE
STATE STANDARD
L.2.1d

Irregular Past Tense Verbs

> **COMMON CORE STATE STANDARD L.2.1d**
> Form and use the past tense of frequently occurring irregular verbs
> (e.g., *sat, hid, told*).

Explain

Write *run, ran* on the board. **Say:** *You know that verbs are action words. They can tell about an action happening now. They can also tell about an action that has already happened, an action that happened in the past. The verb* ran *tells about an action happening now. The verb* ran *tells about an action that happened in the past.*

Say: *You know that you add the letters* -ed *to most verbs to show an action that happened in the past. But some verbs have a special form to show action that happened in the past. You must remember the past tense forms of these types of verbs.*

Model

Write these sentences on the board:

> *I walk now. I walked yesterday.*
> *I hide now. I hid yesterday.*

Point out the *-ed* ending for *walked*. Then point out the special form for the verb *hid*. **Say:** *You must remember the word* hid *to show the past for this special verb.*

Guide Practice

Write the following verbs in a column on the board: *sit, run, hide, tell, see, do, come, go*. Ask volunteers to come to the board to write the past tense of each verb. (sat, ran, hid, told, saw, did, came, went)

Erase the past tense verbs. Then have students copy the column of verbs in their journals and write the past tense of each verb. Review the answers together. Finally, pair students for independent practice. Have them fold their papers in half lengthwise so that the column of past tense verbs is hidden, and take turns quizzing each other.

Name_____ Date_____

COMMON CORE
STATE STANDARD
L.2.1d

Form Irregular Past Tense Verbs

An **irregular past tense verb** is a verb whose past tense is not formed by adding **-d** or **-ed**. You must learn and remember the past tense forms of these verbs.

Today Pedro runs. Yesterday Pedro **ran**.

Today Jill hit the ball. Yesterday Jill **hit** the ball.

Circle the correct past tense form of each verb.

1. hide: hide   hid   hided

2. take: take   taked   took

3. tell: told   tell   telled

4. sit: sat   sitted   sit

5. read: readed   read   red

6. eat: eat   eated   ate

COMMON CORE
STATE STANDARD
L.2.1d

Name_____ Date_____

Form Irregular Past Tense Verbs

Write a word from the box to form the past tense of each underlined verb.

cut	bought	kept
flew	knew	bit

1. The puppy <u>bites</u> his chew toy. _____

2. The girls <u>know</u> how to swim. _____

3. We <u>keep</u> our coats in the closet. _____

4. I <u>cut</u> the paper with scissors. _____

5. The birds <u>fly</u> south for the winter. _____

6. We <u>buy</u> apples at the supermarket. _____

Name_____ Date_____

COMMON CORE
STATE STANDARD
L.2.1d

Form Irregular Past Tense Verbs

Read each verb. Write its past tense form in the correct place in the puzzle.

Across

1. fall

2. have

4. forgive

6. ring

7. understand

10. do

12. light

13. tell

14. go

Down

1. feel

2. hear

3. dig

4. fight

5. ride

8. say

9. drink

11. draw

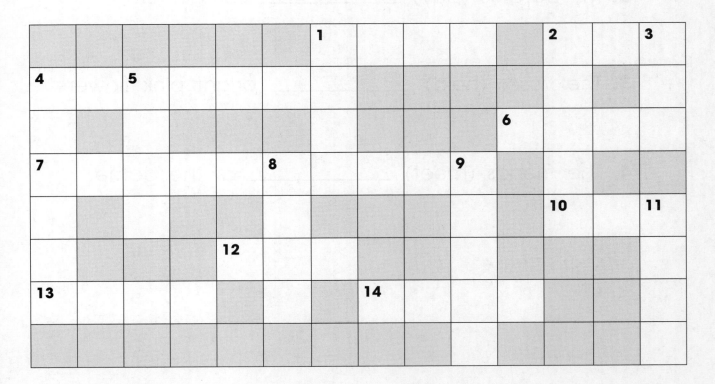

COMMON CORE
STATE STANDARD
L.2.1d

Name_____ Date_____

Use Irregular Past Tense Verbs

An **irregular past tense verb** is a past tense verb that does not end in **-d** or **-ed**.

Present Tense   Past Tense

lose   **lost**

give   **gave**

Write the correct past tense form of the verb in ( ) to complete each sentence.

1. We (find) _____ seashells on the beach.

2. My parents (pay) _____ for dinner.

3. The vases (hold) _____ bright pink flowers.

4. The friends (meet) _____ at the game.

Name_____ Date_____

COMMON CORE
STATE STANDARD
L.2.1d

Use Irregular Past Tense Verbs

Write a sentence for each irregular past tense verb.

1. sang

_____

_____

_____

_____

2. came

_____

_____

_____

_____

3. won

_____

_____

_____

_____

COMMON CORE
STATE STANDARD
L.2.1e

Adjectives and Adverbs

> **COMMON CORE STATE STANDARD L.2.1e**
> Use adjectives and adverbs, and choose between them depending on what is to be modified.

Explain

Tell students that describing words tell about nouns and verbs. **Say:** *Adjectives are describing words that tell about nouns. They can tell how something looks, feels, tastes, smells, or sounds. Adverbs are describing words that tell about verbs. They can tell how, when, or where something happens.*

Explain that students can choose whether to use an adjective or an adverb based on what is being described.

Model

Write the words *soft* and *softly* on the board, along with the following sentences: *I touch the kitten's _____ fur. I _____ touch the kitten's fur.*

Model how to complete each sentence. Explain that since *fur* is a noun, you know to use an adjective to describe it. Guide students to identify that *soft* is an adjective that can tell how a kitten's fur feels. Then explain that since *touch* is a verb, you know to use an adverb to describe it. Guide students to identify that *softly* is an adverb that can tell about how you touch a kitten's fur.

Guide Practice

Display the following words: *nearby, quietly, tiny, carefully, quiet.* Then write the sentences below on the board.

> *The children talk _____ in the library.* (quietly)
> *A _____ bug walks on the leaf.* (tiny)
> *Do you live _____?* (nearby)
> *I could not hear the _____ music.* (quiet)
> *I _____ wash the glass bowl.* (carefully)

Ask a volunteer to choose a word from the list to complete the first sentence. **Ask:** *What kind of describing word did you choose?* (an adverb) *Why?* (because *talk* is a verb and an adverb tells about a verb) Repeat the procedure with the remaining sentences.

Have students write two sentences using describing words to tell about animals and other things they might see at a zoo. Tell them to use at least one adjective and one adverb in their sentences.

Name_____ Date_____

Use Adjectives

> An **adjective** is a word that describes a noun. It can tell how something looks, feels, tastes, smells, or sounds.
>
> The flowers are **pretty**.
>
> The **quiet** mouse hides in a hole.

Circle the adjective in each sentence. Then draw a line under the noun it describes.

1. My blanket is soft.

2. I love to eat spicy food.

3. The elephants are huge.

4. Take out this smelly garbage.

COMMON CORE
STATE STANDARD
L.2.1e

Name_____ Date_____

Use Adjectives

Choose the adjective from the box that best completes each sentence. Write it on the line.

pink	noisy	salty
slippery	heavy	

1. The _____ box was hard to lift.

2. Pretzels are a _____ snack.

3. The wet floor is very _____.

4. We have _____ roses in our garden.

5. The birds were so _____, they woke me up.

Choose two adjectives from the box. Write a sentence for each word.

6. _____

_____

_____

_____

Name_____ Date_____

COMMON CORE
STATE STANDARD
L.2.1e

Use Adverbs

An **adverb** is a word that describes a verb. It can tell how, when, or where something happens.

The band plays **loudly**. (how)

That group will play **later**. (when)

The concert is **outside**. (where)

Circle the adverb in each sentence. Then draw a line under the verb it describes.

1. The girls swing high in the air.

2. Sam quickly climbs the rock wall.

3. I eat downstairs in the kitchen.

4. The children went to the park yesterday.

5. The boys walked slowly to school.

6. We swam in the pool today.

COMMON CORE
STATE STANDARD
L.2.1e

Name_____ Date_____

Use Adverbs

Choose the adverb from the box that best completes each sentence. Write it on the line.

carefully	inside	usually
slowly	soon	

1. The turtle moves _____ across the grass.

2. I _____ go to bed at eight o'clock.

3. Please carry the glass vase _____.

4. The boys came _____ because it was raining.

5. It is noon, so we will eat lunch _____.

Choose two adverbs from the box. Use them in a sentence.

6. _____

_____

_____

_____

Name_____ Date_____

COMMON CORE
STATE STANDARD

L.2.1e

Choose Between Adjectives and Adverbs

> **Adjectives** are words that describe nouns.
> **Adverbs** are words that describe verbs.
>
> The brave firefighter is a hero.
> (The adjective **brave** describes the noun **firefighter**.)
>
> The firefighter ran bravely into the fire.
> (The adverb **bravely** describes the verb **ran**.)

**Circle the adjective or adverb in each sentence.
Then write *adjective* or *adverb* on the line.**

1. The happy baby smiles at her mom.

_____

The baby gurgles happily.

_____

2. Our music teacher sings beautifully.

_____

"America" is a beautiful song.

_____

COMMON CORE
STATE STANDARD
L.2.1e

Name_____ Date_____

Choose Between Adjectives and Adverbs

Circle the word in ( ) that best completes each sentence.

1. The runner (quick / quickly) sprints around the track.

The (quick / quickly) runner crosses the finish line.

2. We heard a (loud / loudly) boom of thunder.

Thunder crashes (loud / loudly) during the storm.

3. Kim was (sleepy / sleepily) at the end of the night.

She yawned (sleepy / sleepily) as she went to bed.

4. The ballet dancer moves (graceful / gracefully).

The star of the show is a (graceful / gracefully)

dancer.

5. Your speech was (clear / clearly).

You spoke (clear / clearly) during your speech.

Name_____ Date_____

COMMON CORE
STATE STANDARD
L.2.1e

Choose Between Adjectives and Adverbs

Read each adjective/adverb pair. Then use each word in a sentence.

1. quiet / quietly

_____

_____

_____

_____

2. careful / carefully

_____

_____

_____

3. slow / slowly

_____

_____

_____

COMMON CORE
STATE STANDARD
L.2.1f

Sentences

> **COMMON CORE STATE STANDARD L.2.1f**
>
> Produce, expand, and rearrange complete simple and compound sentences (e.g., *The boy watched the movie*; *The little boy watched the movie*; *The action movie was watched by the little boy*).

Explain

Tell students that a sentence is a group of words that tells a complete thought. Two types of sentences are simple sentences and compound sentences.

Say: *A simple sentence has a subject and a predicate. The subject, or naming part, tells who or what the sentence is about. The predicate, or telling part, tells what the subject does. You can join two or more simple sentences into a compound sentence using a comma and the word* and, or, *or* but. Explain that good writers use details in their sentences to tell readers exactly what they mean. They also write sentences that are clear and read smoothly. Tell students that they can add, take out, or move words in a sentence to make it clearer.

Model

Write this sentence on the board: *The dog jumped.* Explain that *dog* is the subject and *jumped* is the predicate. Model how to expand the sentence by adding more details. Write this sentence on the board: *The large dog jumped on the couch.* Underline the words you added. **Say:** *You can add details to tell exactly what happened.*

Then **say:** *Sometimes you need to move or take out words to make a sentence clearer.* On the board, write: *The chair was sat on by the cat.* Model how to rearrange the sentence to make it clearer: *The cat sat on the chair.* Explain that by changing the subject, you made the action clear. Then discuss how to form a compound sentence using the two sentences. Model how to join the two sentences using a comma and the word *and*: *The large dog jumped on the sofa, and the cat sat on the chair.*

Guide Practice

Provide students with additional simple sentences. For each, guide them to identify the subject and predicate. Then **ask:** *Is the sentence clear? What words can you add, take out, or move to make the sentence clearer?* Help them expand or rearrange the sentences to make them clearer and smoother to read.

Then write this sentence pair on the board: *The duck quacked. The child ran away.* Tell students to rewrite the sentence as a compound sentence using the word *and*. Then have them add more details to make the sentence more interesting.

Name_____ Date_____

COMMON CORE
STATE STANDARD
L.2.1f

Produce Simple Sentences

A **sentence** tells a complete thought. Every complete sentence has a **subject** and a **predicate**.

- The **subject** is the naming part. It names who or what the sentence is about.
- The **predicate** is the telling part. It tells what the subject does.

Subject: The boys

Predicate: run

Complete Sentence: The boys run.

Read each group of words below. Check *yes* or *no* to tell if it is a complete sentence.

	Yes	No
1. our soccer team	☐	☐
2. Cal bakes bread.	☐	☐
3. walks down the street	☐	☐

COMMON CORE
STATE STANDARD
L.2.1f

Name_____ Date_____

Produce Simple Sentences

Each sentence below is missing a subject or a predicate. Add a subject or a predicate to complete each sentence.

1. My grandma _____.

predicate

2. _____ live in the zoo.

subject

3. The bus driver _____.

predicate

4. _____ won the game!

subject

Write two complete sentences. For each sentence, underline the subject and circle the predicate.

5. _____

_____

_____

6. _____

_____

_____

Name_____ Date_____

Expand Simple Sentences

A sentence is a complete thought.

We saw a movie.

You can add details to a sentence. Details help make its meaning clearer.

We saw a **funny** movie **yesterday**.

Read each sentence. Use words from the box to add more detail. Then write the new sentence on the line.

huge	older	sport
leaves	science	tall

1. The giraffe eats from the tree.

_____

_____

2. What does your brother play?

_____

_____

3. I held a snake at the museum!

_____

_____

COMMON CORE
STATE STANDARD
L.2.1f

Name_____ Date_____

Expand Simple Sentences

Use words or phrases to add details to each sentence. Write the new sentence on the line.

1. Emma wears a scarf.

_____

_____

2. Look at that bug!

_____

_____

3. Our class is taking a trip.

_____

_____

4. Did you see the show?

_____

_____

5. Rico went to the beach.

_____

_____

Name_____ Date_____

Common·Core
State Standard
L.2.1f

Rearrange Simple Sentences

> A good sentence has a clear meaning and reads smoothly. You can move, take out, or add words to make a sentence better.
>
> The lawn mower was pushed by Dad.
>
> **Better:** Dad pushed the lawn mower.

Read each pair of sentences. Circle the sentence that is clearer and smoother.

1. The twins were watched by the babysitter.

The babysitter watched the twins.

2. Lin painted a picture of the sunrise.

A picture of the sunrise was painted by Lin.

3. The problem was solved by Joe!

Joe solved the problem!

4. The escape was made by the zoo animals.

The zoo animals made the escape.

COMMON CORE
STATE STANDARD
L.2.1f

Name_____ Date_____

Rearrange Simple Sentences

Read each sentence. Move and take out words to make the sentence clearer. Write the new sentence on the line.

1. The mountain was climbed by the hikers.

_____

_____

2. This book was read by our class.

_____

_____

3. A new car was bought by Raj.

_____

_____

4. The truck was chased by my dog.

_____

_____

5. These flowers were planted by Mom.

_____

_____

Name_____ Date_____

Produce Compound Sentences

You can join two or more simple sentences into a **compound sentence**. Join the simple sentences by using a comma and the word **and**, **or**, or **but**.

Simple Sentences:
Jay runs fast. Kim runs, too.

Compound Sentence:
Jay runs fast**, and** Kim runs, too.

Read each compound sentence. Write and, *or*, or *but* to complete each sentence.

1. Leo likes strawberries, _____ he does not like blueberries.

2. Should we go to the store now, _____ should we go after dinner?

3. They went to the movies, _____ then they went to the store.

COMMON CORE
STATE STANDARD
L.2.1f

Name_____ Date_____

Produce Compound Sentences

Use *and*, *or*, or *but* to combine each pair of sentences into a compound sentence. Write the new sentence on the line.

1. Sasha went to sleep. Marta stayed up late.

_____

_____

2. I washed the dishes. I took out the garbage.

_____

_____

3. The boys went fishing. They did not catch any fish.

_____

_____

4. Do you want juice? Do you want milk?

_____

_____

Common Core Language Grade 2 • ©2014 Newmark Learning, LLC

Name_____ Date_____

COMMON CORE
STATE STANDARD
L.2.1f

Expand Compound Sentences

A **compound sentence** joins two or more sentences using **and**, **or**, or **but**.

The balloon flew, **and** then it popped.

You can add more detail to a **compound sentence**. Details can give more information and make your meaning clearer.

The balloon flew **away**, and then it popped **loudly**.

Read each compound sentence. Use words from the box to add more detail.

hot	iced	loudly
new	quietly	together

1. Tomas has a _____ game, and we

played it _____.

2. The children talk _____ inside, but they

yell _____ outside.

3. Do you want _____ tea, or do you

want _____ coffee?

COMMON CORE
STATE STANDARD
L.2.1f

Name_____ Date_____

Expand Compound Sentences

Use words or phrases to add more detail to each compound sentence. Write the new sentence on the lines.

1. Mia runs, but her little sister walks.

_____

_____

2. Pick up that chair, and move it over there.

_____

_____

3. Is this your bag, or is that bag yours?

_____

_____

4. Lee pets the cat, and the cat purrs.

_____

_____

COMMON CORE
STATE STANDARD
L.2.1f

Name_____ Date_____

Rearrange Compound Sentences

A good **compound sentence** has a clear meaning and reads smoothly. You can move, take out, or add words to make a sentence clearer.

The car was washed by Jamal, and it was dried by Kevin.

Better: Jamal washed the car, and Kevin dried it.

Read each pair of sentences. Circle the sentence that is clearer.

1. Kelly brought the food, and Sal brought the drinks.

The food was brought by Kelly, and the drinks were brought by Sal.

2. The ball was passed by Manny, and it was caught by Dax.

Manny passed the ball, and Dax caught it.

3. A funny movie was watched by the girls, and a scary movie was watched by the boys.

The girls watched a funny movie, but the boys watched a scary movie.

COMMON CORE
STATE STANDARD

L.2.1f

Name_____ Date_____

Rearrange Compound Sentences

Read each compound sentence. Move and take out words to make it clearer. Write the new sentence on the lines.

1. A picture was colored by the boy, and it was hung up by his mom.

_____

_____

2. The muffins were baked by Grandpa, and the eggs were cooked by Aunt Liz.

_____

_____

3. A blue ribbon was won by Eva, but it was ripped by her cat.

_____

_____

4. The drums were played by Paulo, and the guitar was played by his brother.

_____

_____

Name_____ Date_____

COMMON CORE
STATE STANDARD
L.2.1f

Practice Writing Sentences

Write two simple sentences about a place you have visited.

1. _____

_____

2. _____

_____

Join your two sentences into a compound sentence.

3. _____

_____

Use words or phrases to add more detail to your compound sentence. Write the new sentence on the lines below.

4. _____

_____

_____

Draw a picture to show what you wrote about.

5.

COMMON CORE
STATE STANDARD
L.2.2a

Capitalization

> **COMMON CORE STATE STANDARD L.2.2a**
> Capitalize product names, holidays, and geographic names.

Explain
Tell students that names for holidays, product names, and geographic places must always be capitalized. Capitalizing these words makes clear that they refer to named dates on a calendar, branded products, or exact places on a map.

Say: *You already know that nouns name people, places, and things. Some nouns always begin with a capital letter. The first letter in a holiday, a product name, or an exact place on a map is always capitalized. If there is more than one word in a holiday, exact place, or product name, each word is capitalized.*

Model
Write the following words on the board: *Independence Day*, *Jimmy's Jam*, *California*. Identify each word as a holiday, product name, or exact place, and circle the capital letters in each. Explain that these terms are capitalized because they refer to specific days, products, and places. For example, in the product name above, you are not talking about any type of jam, but a specific brand of jam called Jimmy's Jam.

Guide Practice
Write the following words on the board, with incorrect capitalization as shown: *mother's day*, *pete's pizza*, *new york*, *frosty's fruit ices*, *amazon river*, *thanksgiving*. Guide volunteers to identify the letters in each name that should be capitalized and then rewrite the name correctly.

Then write the following words on the board: *state, river, pizza*. **Ask:** *Do these words have to be capitalized?* (no) *Why not?* (They don't name exact products or places.) Then **ask:** *Would you capitalize each word in the name of our school?* (yes) *Why?* (It is an exact place.) Invite a volunteer to write the name of your school with correct capitalization.

For additional practice, have students write three sentences: one about a favorite holiday, one including a product name, and one about a specific place they have been to. Check that they use proper capitalization in their sentences.

Name_____ Date_____

COMMON CORE
STATE STANDARD
L.2.2a

Capitalize Holidays

A holiday name is a proper noun. Use a **capital letter** for the first letter in the name of a holiday. When a holiday has more than one word, **capitalize** each important word.

Thanksgiving

Fourth of July

Rewrite the name of each holiday correctly.

1. memorial day

_____

2. columbus day

_____

3. mother's day

_____

4. new year's day

_____

COMMON CORE
STATE STANDARD
L.2.2a

Name_____ Date_____

Capitalize Holidays

Read each sentence. Circle the letters that should be capitalized in each holiday name. Write the name correctly on the line.

1. We went to my grandma's house for thanksgiving.

_____

2. My first day of school is after labor Day.

_____

3. We made a Father's day card for our dad.

_____

4. I do not have school on presidents' day.

_____

5. A soldier talked to our class on veterans day.

_____

    Common Core Language Grade 2 • ©2014 Newmark Learning, LLC

Name_____ Date_____

COMMON CORE
STATE STANDARD
L.2.2a

Capitalize Product Names

> **Product names** are proper nouns. Use a capital letter for the first letter in the name of a product. When a product has more than one word, **capitalize** each important word.
>
>
>
> **Spinning Wheels Bicycles**   **Fun Flakes Cereal**

Rewrite the name of each product correctly.

1. Tommy's tricycles

_____

2. grumpy's Granola

_____

3. grassy Farms Yogurt

_____

4. Giant grin Toothpaste

_____

COMMON CORE
STATE STANDARD
L.2.2a

Name_____ Date_____

Capitalize Product Names

Read each sentence. Circle the letters that should be capitalized in each product name. Write the name correctly on the line.

1. My puppy loves Begging bulldog biscuits.

_____

2. Dad cooked dinner with Italy's best pasta.

_____

3. We bought a pack of Bright night Lightbulbs.

_____

Make up a new product and draw it below. Write the name of the product on the line. Be sure to use capital letters correctly.

4.

_____

   Common Core Language Grade 2 • ©2014 Newmark Learning, LLC

Name_____ Date_____

Capitalize Geographic Names

Geographic names, or names of exact places on a map, are proper nouns. Use a **capital letter** for the first letter in the name of an exact place.

Florida

Atlantic Ocean

Rewrite the name of each place correctly.

1. Empire state Building

_____

2. texas

_____

3. Mississippi river

_____

4. rocky Mountains

_____

COMMON CORE
STATE STANDARD
L.2.2a

Name_____ Date_____

Capitalize Geographic Names

Read each sentence. Circle the letters that should be capitalized in each place name. Write the name correctly on the line.

1. We took a trip to the grand Canyon.

_____

2. I live on a street called Pine lane.

_____

3. Ada went swimming in lake Michigan.

_____

4. My cousin lives in chicago.

_____

Write a sentence about an exact place you have been to. Be sure to use capital letters correctly.

5. _____

_____

_____

     Common Core Language Grade 2 • ©2014 Newmark Learning, LLC

Name_____ Date_____

Practice Capitalization

Circle the sentences that use capital letters correctly.

1. We paddled a canoe on lake Washington.

2. We paddled a canoe on Lake Washington.

3. My favorite cereal is Crunchy Oat Flakes.

4. My favorite cereal is crunchy oat flakes.

Draw a picture that shows how you celebrate a holiday. Then write a sentence about it. Be sure to use capital letters correctly.

5.

_____

_____

_____

COMMON CORE
STATE STANDARD
L.2.2b

Commas

> **COMMON CORE STATE STANDARD L.2.2b**
> Use commas in greetings and closings of letters.

Explain

Write a short letter on the board. It should include a greeting followed by a comma, a short body, and a closing with the comma appropriately placed.

Say: *This is a letter. A letter has parts. One part of the letter is the greeting. This is the part where you begin. The greeting starts with a word like* Dear *or* Hello, *followed by the name of the person you are writing to. Then you write a comma after the name.* Point out the greeting in the letter. Circle the comma.

Say: *Another part of a letter is the closing. This is the part where you end the letter. There are two lines in a closing. You write a comma at the end of the first line. The second line is the name or title of the person writing the letter.* Point out the closing. Circle the comma.

Model

Write a sample greeting and closing on the board, without commas. Walk students through the process of adding commas, explaining why you are putting a comma in each place.

Guide Practice

Invite a volunteer to come to the board. Explain that you will dictate a greeting for a letter to a friend. Have the student write the greeting on the board. **Say:** *This is the greeting: Dear Bob.* If necessary, remind the student to write the comma after the name *Bob.* Have the student circle the comma. **Ask:** *Why does a comma belong there?* (because a comma follows the greeting in a letter)

Repeat the activity for a closing with a different volunteer. **Say:** *This is the closing in the letter: Your friend* (pause) *Jan.* If necessary, remind the student to write a comma after the first line of the closing. Have the student circle the comma. **Ask:** *Why does a comma belong there?* (because a comma follows the first line in the closing of a letter)

Write sample greetings and closings on the board, with and without correct punctuation. Ask volunteers to identify if each greeting or closing is written correctly and, if not, to correct it. Then have students write a greeting and a closing in their journals. Remind them to use commas correctly.

Name_____ Date_____

Commas in Greetings

> A **comma** (,) is a punctuation mark with many uses. Use a **comma** in the greeting of a letter. The greeting is a way to say hello. It tells who the letter is for.
>
> Dear Mr. Yee**,**   Dear Aunt Mia**,**

Read each greeting. Check the box if the greeting has the correct punctuation.

1. ☐ Dear Tyrus,

2. ☐ Hello Lucia

3. ☐ Greetings Emma,

4. ☐ Hi Mom,

5. ☐ Dear Chung

6. ☐ Hi Hayden

COMMON CORE
STATE STANDARD
L.2.2b

Name_____ Date_____

Commas in Greetings

Read the greetings. Add any missing commas.

1. May 7, 2015

Dear Will,

I was happy to get your last letter.

2. March 22, 2015

Hi Aisha

I hope everything is great with you and your family.

3. October 9, 2015

Hello Dad

I am having the best time at summer camp.

4. January 25, 2015

Greetings friends

I miss you all and can't wait to see you.

Name_____ Date_____

COMMON CORE
STATE STANDARD
L.2.2b

Commas in Closings

Use a **comma** in the closing of a letter. The closing is a way to say good-bye. It tells who a letter is from.

Best wishes**,**   Your nephew**,**

Emily Hanson   Ben

Read each closing. Check the box if the closing has the correct punctuation.

1. ☐ Your friend,

Sarah

2. ☐ Sincerely

Jim

3. ☐ Love

Mom

4. ☐ Yours truly

Pete

5. ☐ Kind regards

Mr. Ross

6. ☐ Thanks,

Ann

COMMON CORE
STATE STANDARD
L.2.2b

Name_____ Date_____

Commas in Closings

Read each closing. Add any missing commas.

1. Your friend

Tara

2. Sincerely,

Jose

3. Regards

Uncle Bill

4. Thanks

The Martins

5. Yours truly,

Raina

6. Love

Mom

7. Best wishes

Ed

8. Best

Ms. Wilde's Class

9. Fondly,

Elena

10. Thank you

Mr. Wu

Common Core Language Grade 2 • ©2014 Newmark Learning, LLC

Name_____ Date_____

Commas in Greetings and Closings

Write a greeting and a closing for each letter. Be sure to use commas correctly.

1. May 12, 2015

_____

My new puppy is here. Come visit us soon!

_____

Olivia

2. November 5, 2015

_____

We can't wait to see you at Thanksgiving.

_____

Jack

COMMON CORE
STATE STANDARD
L.2.2c

Apostrophes

> **COMMON CORE STATE STANDARD L.2.2c**
> Use an apostrophe to form contractions and frequently occurring possessives.

Explain

Say: *You can put two short words together to form a contraction.* Write *do not* on the board. Below *do not*, write *don't*. **Say:** *You use an apostrophe to take the place of one or more letters when you put the words together.* Point out that the *o* in *not* was taken out when the words *do* and *not* were put together, and the apostrophe takes the place of the missing *o*.

Next, write these sentences on the board: *The teacher has a pencil. It is the teacher's pencil.* Read the sentences aloud, having students repeat. **Say:** *A noun names a person, place, or thing. Some kinds of nouns can show that someone has something. In this sentence, the apostrophe and letter* s *after the noun* teacher *show that the teacher has the pencil.* Circle the apostrophe as you name it.

Model

Write these sentence pairs on the board:

> *The child has a wagon. It is the child's wagon.*
> *The cats have a toy. It is the cats' toy.*

Circle each apostrophe. **Say:** *In the first sentence, the wagon belongs to only one child. If you are writing about one person, place, or thing, write the apostrophe before the letter* s. *In the second sentence, the toys belong to many cats. If you are writing about more than one person, place, or thing, write the apostrophe after the letter* s.

To model contraction use, write *is not* and *isn't* on the board. Identify *isn't* as a contraction and circle the apostrophe. **Ask:** *Why did I write an apostrophe in the word* isn't? (The apostrophe takes the place of the letter *o* in *not*.)

Guide Practice

Write the following sentence pairs on the board. Do not write the answers in parentheses.

> *The children have a basketball. It is the _____ basketball.* (children's)
> *The two men have a car. It is the _____ car.* (men's)

Have students complete each second sentence, circle the apostrophe, and explain why they used it. Then write *did not, have not,* and *was not* on the board. Work with students to form contractions from each pair of words (didn't, haven't, wasn't). Have students write each contraction, circle each apostrophe, and explain why they used it.

Name_____ Date_____

COMMON CORE
STATE STANDARD
L.2.2c

Apostrophes in Contractions

An **apostrophe** (') is a punctuation mark.
Use an **apostrophe** in a contraction to take
the place of the missing letter or letters.

    should not = shouldn't

    she is = she's

**Draw a line to match each pair of words with its
contraction.**

1. it is   **a.** they'll

2. can not   **b.** it's

3. I am   **c.** you're

4. you are   **d.** can't

5. they will   **e.** I'm

COMMON CORE
STATE STANDARD
L.2.2c

Name_____ Date_____

Apostrophes in Contractions

**Write the contraction for each underlined pair
of words.**

1. <u>It is</u> your turn to do the dishes.

2. <u>You had</u> better give my hat back.

3. I <u>did not</u> take your hat!

4. <u>I am</u> leaving for school now.

5. <u>We will</u> pick you up.

6. <u>They are</u> on the soccer team.

7. <u>She is</u> really good at math.

8. I <u>could not</u> eat another bite!

           Common Core Language Grade 2 • ©2014 Newmark Learning, LLC

Name_____ Date_____

Apostrophes in Possessives

> Use an **apostrophe** to form a **possessive noun**. A **possessive noun** shows who owns or has something.
>
> - Add **'s** to a singular noun.
>   a friend**'s** house
> - Add an **apostrophe** after the **s** in a plural noun.
>   all of the student**s'** books
> - If a plural noun does not end in **s**, add **'s**.
>   the children**'s** toys

Circle the correct possessive form.

1. the games Tom owns

Toms' games   Tom's games

2. the toys the girls have

the girl's toys   the girls' toys

3. the shirts the men have

the men's shirts   the mens' shirts

4. the pets the kids own

the kid's pets   the kids' pets

COMMON CORE
STATE STANDARD
L.2.2c

Name_____ Date_____

Apostrophes in Possessives

Rewrite each sentence. Use a possessive noun to replace each underlined phrase.

1. <u>The apple Gwen has</u> is red.

_____

2. <u>The car that the women have</u> needs to be fixed.

_____

3. <u>The rules of the parents</u> were tough.

_____

4. <u>The houses that the people own</u> will be sold today.

_____

Common Core Language Grade 2 • ©2014 Newmark Learning, LLC

Name_____ Date_____

COMMON CORE
STATE STANDARD
L.2.2c

Apostrophes in Contractions and Possessives

Rewrite each underlined word so that it uses an apostrophe correctly.

1. <u>Bens</u> birthday party is today.

_____

2. I <u>cant</u> go.

_____

3. His best <u>friends</u> gift is a new basketball.

_____

4. Both of our <u>parents</u> cars are blue.

_____

5. The <u>cats</u> name is Mister Pancake.

_____

6. <u>Theyll</u> bring it home tomorrow.

_____

COMMON CORE
STATE STANDARD
L.2.2d

Spelling Patterns

> **COMMON CORE STATE STANDARD L.2.2d**
> Generalize learned spelling patterns when writing words (e.g., *cage*, *badge*; *boy*, *boil*).

Explain

Tell students that a spelling pattern is a group of letters that stands for a sound. The same spelling patterns appear in many words, so knowing spelling patterns can help students figure out how to decode and spell words.

Say: *When you know the sounds that different spelling patterns stand for, you can find these sounds in new words, and figure out how to say and write them.*

Model

Write the following spelling patterns on the board: *oi, oy*. Then write the words *boy* and *boil*. **Say:** *The letters* oy *make a spelling pattern. These two letters stand for the sound /oy/, like in the word* boy. *The letters* oi *make another spelling pattern. It has the same sound as* oy. *This spelling pattern is found in the word* boil *and many other* oi *words.*

Repeat the words *boy* and *boil* as you point to each one so that students can identify that the same vowel sound appears in each.

Guide Practice

Next to the *oy/oi* spelling patterns, write the following spelling patterns on the board: *ge, dge*. Then write the words *cage* and *badge*. **Say:** *The letters* ge *and the* dge *are spelling patterns that make the soft* g *sound: /j/.* Have students repeat the /j/ sound and each word after you. **Ask:** *Do the words* cage *and* badge *have the same* /j/ *sound?* (yes)

Now write the following words on the board: *coil, spoil, joy, soy, stage, age, edge, hedge*. Ask students to write the words down in their notebooks. **Say:** *I can use what I know about the spelling pattern* oi *to figure out how to say the first word:* coil. Have students repeat the word after you.

Guide volunteers to point to the *oi, oy, ge,* and *dge* spelling patterns in the remaining words. Have them say each spelling pattern and then each word aloud. Then have the entire class repeat each word and underline its *oy, oi, ge,* or *dge* spelling pattern in their notebooks.

Name_____ Date_____

COMMON CORE
STATE STANDARD
L.2.2d

Spelling Patterns: oy/oi, dge/ge

Use **spelling patterns** to learn how to spell new words.

- In words with the vowel teams **oy** and **oi**, two letters work together to make the same vowel sound.

boy   **boil**

- The letters **dge** and **ge** make the **/j/** or soft **g** sound.

badge   **cage**

Use **dge** to spell words with a short vowel sound.
Use **ge** to spell words with a long vowel sound.

Say the words for each item. Circle the two words that have the same sound.

1. toy   coin   foot

2. page   sing   bridge

COMMON CORE
STATE STANDARD
L.2.2d

Name_____ Date_____

Spelling Patterns: CVC and CVCe

- In words with the **Consonant-Vowel-Consonant** (CVC) pattern, the vowel sound is short.

- In words with the **Consonant-Vowel-Consonant-e** (CVCe) pattern, the vowel sound is long and the **e** is silent.

- Add silent **e** to the end of a CVC word to change the vowel sound from short to long.

  cap + **e** = cap**e**   pin + **e** = pin**e**
  CVC + **e** = CVC**e**   CVC + **e** = CVC**e**

Circle the word that names each picture.

1.   tap   tape

2.   kit   kite

3.   tub   tube

4.   fin   fine

5.   can   cane

   Common Core Language Grade 2 • ©2014 Newmark Learning, LLC

Name_____ Date_____

Spelling Patterns: ch, sh

Reach each sentence. Write *ch* or *sh* to complete each word that has missing letters.

1. Please _____ut the door.

2. I put on my new _____irt.

3. The young _____ild played on the slide.

4. Look at that _____ip sailing away!

5. Let's eat our lun_____ outside today!

6. I sat in my favorite _____air and read.

COMMON CORE
STATE STANDARD
L.2.2e

Use Reference Materials for Spelling

> **COMMON CORE STATE STANDARD L.2.2e**
> Consult reference materials, including beginning dictionaries, as needed to check and correct spellings.

Explain

Tell students that they can use reference materials to check and correct the spelling of a word. **Say:** *Reference materials you can use include glossaries, dictionaries, spellcheckers on a computer, and printed classroom materials such as posters and calendars.*

Model

Display this sample text from a page in a dictionary.

---

flounce
flour [FLOW-er]
    (noun) finely ground, sifted grain used in baking
flow
flower [FLOW-er]
    (noun) a blossom that blooms on a plant
    (verb) to produce flowers

Say: *Let's say you want to write the word* flour *in a recipe, but you're not sure how to spell it. Here's how you can use a dictionary to figure it out. Start by looking for the first letters* f-l-o *in the dictionary. Once you find a word you think is right, read the definition. Here, the word* flour *is a "grain used in baking," so that is the word you want. Now you can spell it,* f-l-o-u-r. Explain that *flower* would be incorrect because the meaning does not make sense for a recipe. **Say:** *Now you want to write about a flower blossom. What is the correct spelling?* (flower)

Guide Practice

Pair students and provide books with glossaries and/or print and online dictionaries. Dictate the words *energy, surface, napkin,* and *clumsy*. Work with the class to find the definition and correct spelling of the first word, and then have pairs use their reference materials to write the correct spelling of each remaining word, and also find its definition. Repeat each word as often as necessary, and check that partners find the correct definitions and spellings.

Name_____ Date_____

Use Reference Materials for Spelling

You can use **reference materials**, such as a dictionary, to check the spelling of a word.

Sample Dictionary

eyesight (noun) the ability to see

grumble (verb) to complain

lax (adjective) not strict

palace (noun) a large home for a king or queen

remove (verb) to take away

vast (adjective) huge

Use the sample dictionary above to check the spelling of the words. If the word is spelled correctly, circle it. If it is misspelled, write the correct spelling.

1. eyesite

_____

2. laks

_____

3. palace

_____

4. remoove

_____

COMMON CORE
STATE STANDARD
L.2.3a

Formal and Informal English

> **COMMON CORE STATE STANDARD L.2.3a**
> Compare formal and informal uses of English.

Explain

Tell students that informal English is what people use when they talk to their friends and family. Formal English is what people use when they speak to people they don't know very well, or make a presentation at work or school.

Say: *Informal English is a casual way of talking. If you say, "Hey, what's up?" that's informal English. Formal English is less casual. If you say, "Hello, how are you today?" that's formal English. You would use formal English to speak to the principal of the school and informal English to talk to your brother.*

Model

Tell students that you want to write a letter to your town's mayor about an idea you do not agree with. Then write the following sentences on the board: *This is the worst idea ever! I strongly disagree with this idea.* Identify which is formal and which is informal. **Say:** *I will use the second sentence in my letter because I don't know the mayor and I want him or her to take me seriously.*

Guide Practice

Write the following sentences and scenarios on the board:

giving a speech to strangers	I appreciate your time and attention.
	Thanks a million for listening, guys.
an e-mail to your best friend	I look forward to your arrival.
	Can't wait to see you!
a letter to your local newspaper	I'm writing to tell you that this plan is totally nuts.
	I wish to express my concern about this issue.

Work through the first example with students, prompting them to identify which sentence is formal and which is informal, and then tell which is more appropriate for the situation. Have partners work through the remaining examples together. Go over the answers as a class.

Name_____ Date_____

Common Core
State Standard
L.2.3a

Formal and Informal English

> **Informal English** is a way of speaking that you might use to talk to your friends or family. **Formal English** is what you might use when writing a report or talking to someone you don't know very well.
>
> | **Informal** | **Formal** |
> |---|---|
> | Hey! What's up? | Hello. How are you? |

Read each sentence. Write *informal* or *formal* on the line to tell what kind of sentence it is.

1. Thank you very much for your time.

_____

2. Yup, sounds good to me!

_____

3. We all enjoyed ourselves at the concert.

_____

4. I'll shoot you an e-mail about the party.

_____

COMMON CORE
STATE STANDARD
L.2.3a

Name_____ Date_____

Formal and Informal English

Read each informal statement. Rewrite it as a formal statement.

1. Yo, cool shoes!

_____

_____

_____

2. We had a totally awesome day at the zoo.

_____

_____

_____

Read the formal statement. Rewrite it as an informal statement.

3. I look forward to seeing you both tomorrow.

_____

_____

_____

Common Core Language Grade 2 • ©2014 Newmark Learning, LLC

Lesson Plan Teacher Worksheet

Vocabulary Acquisition and Use

The lessons in this section are organized in the same order as the Common Core Language Standards for vocabulary acquisition and use. Each mini-lesson provides specific, explicit instruction for a Language standard and is followed by multiple practice pages. Use the following chart to track the standards students have practiced. You may wish to revisit mini-lessons and practice pages a second time for spiral review.

Common Core State Standards	Mini-Lessons and Practice	Page	Complete (✓)	Review (✓)
L.2.4a	Mini-Lesson 13: Context Clues	78		
	Practice Pages: Context Clues	79		
L.2.4b	Mini-Lesson 14: Prefixes	82		
	Practice Pages: Prefixes	83		
L.2.4c	Mini-Lesson 15: Roots	86		
	Practice Pages: Roots	87		
L.2.4d	Mini-Lesson 16: Compound Words	90		
	Practice Pages: Compound Words	91		
L.2.4e	Mini-Lesson 17: Use Glossaries and Dictionaries	94		
	Practice Pages: Use Glossaries and Dictionaries	95		
L.2.5a	Mini-Lesson 18: Make Connections	98		
	Practice Pages: Make Connections	99		
L.2.5b	Mini-Lesson 19: Distinguish Shades of Meaning	102		
	Practice Pages: Distinguish Shades of Meaning	103		
	Answer Key	126		

COMMON CORE
STATE STANDARD
L.2.4a

Context Clues

> **COMMON CORE STATE STANDARD L.2.4a**
> Use sentence-level context as a clue to the meaning of a word or phrase.

Explain

Tell students that context clues are words they can use to figure out the meaning of unknown words.

Say: *When you are reading and come across a word you don't know, you can use context clues to figure out its meaning. Context clues are words you know that can give you an idea of what a word you don't know might mean.*

Model

Write the following sentence on the board and read it aloud:

> *I scalded my tongue on the hot soup.*

Say: *I can use context clues to figure out what the word* scalded *means. I look at the words* tongue *and* hot soup. *I know that the word* scalded *tells what happens when someone's tongue touches very hot soup. I think the word* scalded *must mean "burned."*

Guide Practice

Write the following sentences on the board and underline as shown:

> *The glass vase is delicate, so be <u>careful not to break it</u>.*
> *The sparrow <u>flew</u> to its nest in the <u>tree</u> and <u>sang a song</u>.*
> *The cup is <u>empty</u> so I will refill it with water.*

Circle the words *delicate*, *sparrow*, and *refill*. Explain that these are the words students have to figure out. Then explain that the underlined words are context clues for the circled words. Guide students to use these context clues to figure out the first unknown word. For example, for the first sentence, **ask:** *When might you have to be careful not to break something?* (when it is something that breaks easily) *What do you know about things made of glass?* (They can break if you drop them.) *What do you think the word* delicate *means?* (easy to break or harm)

Have partners work together to find the meaning of the unknown words in the second and third sentences. Then go over the sentences as a class.

Name_____ Date_____

COMMON CORE
STATE STANDARD
L.2.4a

Context Clues

When you see a word you don't know, you can use **context clues** to figure out its meaning. In the sentence below, the words **served** and **food** are clues to the meaning of **platter**.

We **served** the **food** on a **platter**.

A **platter** is a large plate used for serving food.

Read each sentence. Use the underlined context clues. Then circle the meaning of the bold word.

1. The **huge** bowl of pasta fed our <u>whole family</u>.

      small   large   red

2. The room is so **cluttered** I <u>can't even see the floor</u>!

      large   messy   clean

3. I will **tear** the paper into <u>two pieces</u> so we can both draw.

      paint   glue   rip

COMMON CORE
STATE STANDARD
L.2.4a

Name_____ Date_____

Context Clues

Read each sentence. Use the underlined context clues to find the meaning of the boldfaced word. Write the meaning on the line.

1. I watched the <u>ball</u> **bounce** <u>up and down</u> on the <u>hard floor</u>.

_____

2. The **enormous** suitcase <u>does not fit</u> into the car.

_____

3. I watched the boat **float** <u>on top of</u> the <u>water</u>.

_____

4. I like all the <u>books</u> this **author** has <u>written</u>.

_____

5. We can use a <u>net</u> to **capture** fish.

_____

Name_____ Date_____

Context Clues

Use context clues to find the meaning of each boldfaced word. Write the meaning on the line. Underline the context clues you used.

1. Let's talk in a **whisper** so we don't wake up the baby.

_____

2. I couldn't stop laughing at the **hilarious** movie.

_____

3. We made a hole in the **soil** to plant the seeds in.

_____

4. My hair blew back and forth on the **blustery** day.

_____

COMMON CORE
STATE STANDARD
L.2.4b

Prefixes

> **COMMON CORE STATE STANDARD L.2.4b**
> Determine the meaning of a new word formed when a known prefix
> is added to a known word (e.g., *happy/unhappy, tell/retell*).

Explain

Tell students that a prefix is a group of letters at the beginning of a word that
changes the word's meaning. **Say:** *When you know the meanings of prefixes,
you can use them to figure out the meanings of new words.*

Model

Write *happy* and *unhappy* on the board, and underline the prefix *un-*.
Say: *You can see that* unhappy *is the word* happy *with the prefix* un- *at
the beginning. The prefix* un- *means "not," so it changes the meaning
to "not happy."*

Then display the following prefix chart. **Say:** *This chart shows the meaning
of some common prefixes.* Point out the word *unhappy* in the first row of
the chart.

Prefix	Meaning	Example
un-	not, opposite of	unhappy
re-	again, back	retell
mis-	wrongly	misspell
pre-	before	preschool

Then point out the word *retell* in the chart. Ask students to identify the prefix
in the word (re-) and circle it. **Say:** *Let's say I read the word* retell*, but I'm not
sure what it means. I can see that* retell *is formed from the prefix* re- *and the
word* tell*:* re- + tell = retell*. I know what the word* tell *means, and I know that
the prefix* re- *means "again." Now I can figure out that* retell *means "to tell
again."*

Follow a similar procedure to discuss the remaining examples on the chart.

Guide Practice

Write the following words on the board: *rebuild, unsafe, mistreat, precook*.
Have volunteers circle the prefix in each word, tell what the prefix means, and
then use the prefix to explain the meaning of the word. Then add each word
to the chart.

COMMON CORE
STATE STANDARD
L.2.4b

Name_____ Date_____

Prefixes

A **prefix** is a word part that is added to the beginning of a base word. It changes the meaning of the base word.

re- means "again" **re-** + **heat** = reheat

un- means "not" **un-** + **lock** = unlock

Circle the prefix in each word. Then write the meaning of the whole word on the line.

1. rethink _____

2. unfair _____

3. review _____

4. untrue _____

5. reread _____

6. unclear _____

COMMON CORE
STATE STANDARD
L.2.4b

Name_____ Date_____

Prefixes

> A **prefix** is a word part that is added to the beginning of a base word. It changes the meaning of the base word.
>
> **mis-** means "wrongly"   **mis-** + **step** = misstep
> **pre-** means "before"   **pre-** + **pay** = prepay

Add a prefix from the box to each word. Then draw a line to its meaning.

re-	un-	mis-	pre-

1. _____spell   **a.** pack again

2. _____heat   **b.** count wrongly

3. _____pack   **c.** spell wrongly

4. _____kind   **d.** test before

5. _____count   **e.** heat before

6. _____test   **f.** not kind

Name_____ Date_____

COMMON CORE
STATE STANDARD
L.2.4b

Prefixes

Find the word with the prefix and underline it. Then circle the meaning of the word.

1. Dad has to repaint the cracked wall.

    paint again   paint before

2. Chewing furniture is one way our dogs misbehave.

    behave well   behave badly

3. It is unfair that I have to go to bed before Anna!

    not fair   more fair

4. My parents preview movies before we see them.

    watch before   watch again

5. We felt unlucky when we just missed the bus.

    very lucky   not lucky

6. Sara's mom asked her to remake the bed.

    make again   make before

COMMON CORE
STATE STANDARD
L.2.4c

Roots

> **COMMON CORE STATE STANDARD L.2.4c**
> Use a known root word as a clue to the meaning of an unknown
> word with the same root (e.g., *addition*, *additional*).

Explain

Tell students that a root word is a basic word that can be used to form larger
words. **Say:** *When you know the meanings of root words, you can use them
to figure out the meanings of words that have the same root.*

Model

Write *fear* and *fearful* on the board, and underline the root word *fear* in each
word. **Say:** *You can see that the word* fearful *is the root word* fear *with the
ending* -ful. *You can use the meaning of* fear *("a scared feeling") to figure out
the meaning of* fearful. *The word* fearful *means "full of fear" or "very scared."*

Then display this chart. **Say:** *This chart shows words that combine root words
and common endings.* Point out the word *fearful* in the first row of the chart.

Word	Root + Ending	Meaning
fearful	fear + -ful	full of fear, very scared
useless	use + -less	without a use
illness	ill + -ness	state of being sick

Then point out the word *useless*. Ask students to identify the root word (use)
and underline it. **Say:** *Suppose I read the word* useless, *but I'm not sure what
it means. I can see that* useless *is formed from the root word* use *and the
ending* -less: use + -less = useless. *I know that the word* use *means "what
something does or is good for" and that the ending* -less *means "without."
Now I can figure out that* useless *means "without a use, or doing nothing."*

Follow a similar procedure to discuss the remaining example on the chart.

Guide Practice

Write the following words on the board: *painful, homeless, sadness.* Have
volunteers underline the root word in each word, and then use the root
word and ending to figure out the word's meaning. Then add each word to
the chart.

Name_____ Date_____

COMMON CORE
STATE STANDARD
L.2.4c

Roots

A **root word** is a base word without prefixes or suffixes. Remember that a **prefix** is a word part that comes before a base word. A **suffix** is a word part that comes after.

Suffixes

-al   relating to, or having to do with

-er   a person who

-ness the state of

Draw lines to match the words that have the same root.

1. walker   **a.** emotional

2. sicker   **b.** camp

3. magical   **c.** darker

4. camper   **d.** magic

5. darkness   **e.** walk

6. emotion   **f.** sickness

COMMON CORE
STATE STANDARD
L.2.4c

Name_____ Date_____

Roots

> Combining a **root word** and a **suffix** makes a new word.
>
> **hope** + **-ful** = hopeful (full of hope)
>
> You can use the **root** and **suffix** to tell a word's meaning.
>
> fearless = **fear** + **-less** (without fear)

Circle the root and underline the suffix in each word. Then complete the definition.

1. sadness   state of being _____

2. colorful   full of _____

3. careless   without _____

4. player   person who _____

5. helpless   without _____

6. cheerful   full of _____

7. farmer   person who _____

Common Core Language Grade 2 • ©2014 Newmark Learning, LLC

Name_____ Date_____

Roots

Write a definition for the underlined word. Use the root and suffix to figure out what it means.

1. My <u>helpful</u> dog brought me my shoes.

_____

_____

2. Our <u>teacher</u> never misses a day of school.

_____

_____

3. The <u>illness</u> made my throat hurt.

_____

_____

4. The dessert had <u>seasonal</u> fruits, like watermelon.

_____

_____

5. Ella's <u>wireless</u> Internet connection is very fast.

_____

_____

Compound Words

> **COMMON CORE STATE STANDARD L.2.4d**
> Use knowledge of the meaning of individual words to predict the meaning of compound words (e.g., *birdhouse, lighthouse, housefly; bookshelf, notebook, bookmark*).

Explain
Tell students that a compound word is a word made up of two smaller words. **Say:** *You can use what you know about smaller words to figure out the meaning of compound words.*

Model
Write *book, shelf,* and *bookshelf* on the board. **Say:** *You can see that* bookshelf *is made up of the words* book *and* shelf. *You can use what you know about the meanings of* book *and* shelf *to figure out that a bookshelf is a shelf that people put books on.*

Then display the following prefix chart. **Say:** *This chart shows the meaning of some compound words.* Point out the word bookshelf in the first row of the chart.

Word	+	Word	=	Compound Word	Meaning
book		shelf		bookshelf	a shelf for books
house		boat		houseboat	a boat that acts as a house
basket		ball		basketball	a ball that goes into a basket
waste		paper		wastepaper	paper that is trash, or waste

Then point out the word *houseboat* in the chart. Ask students to identify the two words that make it up (house, boat). **Say:** *Let's say I read the word* houseboat, *but I'm not sure what it means. I see that* houseboat *is formed from the words* house *and* boat: house + boat = houseboat. *I know what the words* house *and* boat *mean, so I know that a houseboat is a boat that acts as a house, or a boat that someone lives in.*

Follow a similar procedure to discuss the remaining examples on the chart.

Guide Practice
Write the following words on the board: *doormat, baseball, bookstore, newspaper.* Have volunteers identify the words that make up each compound word, and then use those words to explain the meaning of the compound word.

Name_____ Date_____

COMMON CORE
STATE STANDARD
L.2.4d

Compound Words

A **compound word** is a word made up of two smaller words. The smaller words can help you figure out the meaning of the **compound word**.

**bird + house
= birdhouse**

**book + shelf
= bookshelf**

Join the two small words to make a new compound word. Write the compound word on the line.

1. skate + board = _____

2. tooth + brush = _____

3. star + fish = _____

4. side + walk = _____

5. fire + fly = _____

COMMON CORE
STATE STANDARD
L.2.4d

Name_____ Date_____

Compound Words

Circle the compound word in each sentence. Write the two words that make up the compound word on the lines.

1. Greta played outside all day on Saturday.

_____   _____

2. Sam and Jill ate pancakes this morning.

_____   _____

3. Dad bakes tasty blueberry muffins.

_____   _____

4. The waves wash away the footprints in the sand.

_____   _____

5. The students carry their books in backpacks.

_____   _____

6. After the storm, there was a rainbow in the sky.

_____   _____

Common Core Language Grade 2 • ©2014 Newmark Learning, LLC

Name_____ Date_____

COMMON CORE
STATE STANDARD
L.2.4d

Compound Words

Replace the underlined word in each compound word with a word from the box. Write the new compound word on the line. Then draw a picture to show the new word you wrote.

| basket | rain | pack | glasses |

1. back<u>yard</u>

_____

2. <u>foot</u>ball

_____

3. <u>over</u>coat

_____

4. sun<u>light</u>

_____

COMMON CORE
STATE STANDARD
L.2.4e

Use Glossaries and Dictionaries

> **COMMON CORE STATE STANDARD L.2.4e**
> Use glossaries and beginning dictionaries, both print and digital, to determine or clarify the meaning of words and phrases.

Explain

Tell students that they can use a glossary or dictionary to find or check the meaning of a word. Explain that a dictionary is a stand-alone resource, either print or digital, and that a glossary often appears at the end of another text and lists the difficult words from that text. Remind students that when they have only a pretty good idea of what a word means, they should check to be very sure.

Model

Display this sample text from a dictionary.

cres•cent [KREH-sent]
(noun) a curved shape like the moon when it is just a sliver in the sky

Say: *Suppose you want to describe a crescent moon in a poem, but you're not exactly sure what it means. Here's how you can use a dictionary to figure it out. Find the word* crescent *in the alphabetical list in the dictionary. Then read the definition to understand exactly what the word means. Sometimes, there is more than one definition and you have to figure out which one you want.*

Display an online dictionary and show how to type the word *crescent* into the search box. Point out the importance of spelling the word correctly, or getting very close, as some online dictionaries will find only the exact spelling of the word, while others will find spellings close to a misspelled word. Then read the results together.

If available, share a book about the moon where the word *crescent* appears boldfaced in the text and as an entry in the glossary. **Say:** *Boldfaced type may mean that a word is defined in the glossary.*

Guide Practice

Pair students and provide books with glossaries, beginning dictionaries, and online dictionaries if possible. Write the words *mass, triangle, famous,* and *rumor* on the board. Find the first word as a class, having volunteers walk you through the steps of looking it up in a dictionary or glossary. Then have pairs use their reference materials to find and write the meaning of each remaining word.

Common Core Language Grade 2 • ©2014 Newmark Learning, LLC

Name_____ Date_____

COMMON CORE
STATE STANDARD
L.2.4e

Use a Glossary

A **glossary** is a list of the hard or unusual words found in a book. It lists the words in alphabetical order and tells what they mean.

Butterfly Life Cycle Glossary

adult: when the butterfly is fully grown

egg: first stage in the life cycle

larva: stage between egg and pupa; looks like a worm

pupa: stage between larva and adult; covered by a shell

Read the definitions in the glossary. Then circle the correct answer to the questions below.

1. Which stage comes first?

adult   egg

2. What stage comes after the egg?

larva   pupa

3. When is a butterfly covered with a shell?

egg   pupa

4. What is the last stage?

larva   adult

COMMON CORE
STATE STANDARD
L.2.4e

Name_____ Date_____

Use a Dictionary

A **dictionary** gives information about words. Each entry tells a word's meaning, spelling, and part of speech. It also tells you how to say the word. The words are listed in alphabetical order. A **dictionary** can be a book or an online resource.

limb (LIM) noun

a part of a body used in grasping and holding

a branch of a tree

Use a print or online dictionary to find the meaning of each word on the left. Draw lines to match each word to its definition.

1. reject   **a.** drops of water

2. dew   **b.** quick to notice and act

3. peculiar   **c.** refuse to accept

4. alert   **d.** strange or unusual

          Common Core Language Grade 2 • ©2014 Newmark Learning, LLC

Name_____ Date_____

COMMON CORE
STATE STANDARD
L.2.4e

Use Glossaries and Dictionaries

Use a print or online glossary or dictionary to find the meaning of each word. Write the meaning on the lines.

1. gash

_____

_____

2. delight

_____

_____

3. intrude

_____

_____

4. motion

_____

_____

COMMON CORE
STATE STANDARD
L.2.5a

Make Connections

> **COMMON CORE STATE STANDARD L.2.5a**
> Identify real-life connections between words and their use (e.g.,
> describe foods that are spicy or juicy).

Explain

Tell students that knowing how to use the right word for something, or
identifying the connections between words and their uses, will help them
describe what they see, hear, smell, taste, and experience in an accurate and
effective way.

Say: *You can use what you know from your everyday life to describe sights,
smells, tastes, sounds, and experiences. It's important to choose your
describing words carefully. For example, you might describe tacos as spicy
and peaches as juicy, but you wouldn't describe tacos as juicy and peaches
as spicy!*

Model

Write the word *roar* on the board with four lines extending from it. **Say:** Roar
*is a word that describes a kind of low, loud sound. I will think about things
I know that roar.* Write the following words for each of the four lines: *lion,
motorcycle, ocean, lawn mower.*

Say: *I can use the word* roar *to describe things that make a low, loud sound—
like a motorcycle or a lawnmower. I would not use it to describe soft or high
sounds, such as the sounds that a mouse, a xylophone, or bells make.*

Guide Practice

Copy the following chart onto the board.

Word	What It Describes	What It Does Not Describe
noisy		
sweet		
fuzzy		
rough		

Guide students to name several things you could accurately describe using
each word. For example, a vacuum cleaner is noisy, watermelon is sweet,
a tennis ball is fuzzy, and the sidewalk is rough. Challenge students to also
name one thing that each word does not describe.

Name_____ Date_____

COMMON CORE
STATE STANDARD
L.2.5a

Make Connections

Making connections between words and their uses can help you use just the right word to describe something. All the words below describe tastes and smells, but they don't all mean the same thing!

I ate a **juicy** orange. (full of juice)

The pepper was **spicy**. (having a hot, strong taste)

The fire had a **smoky** smell. (smelling like smoke)

The garbage was **stinky**. (smelling bad)

Choose the taste or smell word from the box that best describes each thing. Write it on the line.

| juicy | spicy | smoky | stinky |

1. peach _____

2. old cheese _____

3. chili _____

4. campfire _____

COMMON CORE
STATE STANDARD
L.2.5a

Name_____ Date_____

Make Connections

Read each taste or smell word and its meaning. Decide which word is best for each sentence and write it on the line.

Smells	Tastes
fresh — smelling clean and new **smelly** — having a bad smell **fragrant** — having a nice smell **piney** — smelling like pine trees	**salty** — tasting like salt **tasty** — having a good taste **tasteless** — having no taste **sweet** — tasting like sugar

1. Does watermelon taste salty or sweet?

_____

2. Do clean clothes smell fresh or smelly?

_____

3. Is your favorite food tasty or tasteless?

_____

4. Do roses smell fragrant or piney?

_____

Name_____ Date_____

Make Connections

All of the words in the box name different kinds of homes. Read each word and its meaning. Then write the correct word next to each person or animal.

---

hive — a place where bees live

den — home for some kinds of wild animals

cabin — small, simple house that is usually in the country

apartment — one or more rooms in a larger building

palace — a very large, fancy home where rulers or other important people may live

---

1. a king _____

2. someone who wants to spend a week in the country _____

3. a family of foxes _____

4. someone who wants to live in a tall building _____

5. a honeybee _____

COMMON CORE
STATE STANDARD
L.2.5b

Distinguish Shades of Meaning

> **COMMON CORE STATE STANDARD L.2.5b**
>
> Distinguish shades of meaning among closely related verbs (e.g., *toss, throw, hurl*) and closely related adjectives (e.g., *thin, slender, skinny, scrawny*).

Explain

Tell students that shades of meaning are the small differences between words that are related. Both verbs and adjectives can have shades of meaning.

Say: *Two words might have similar meanings, but one of the words may have a stronger meaning. Think about the words* mad *and* furious. *The word* furious *has a more powerful meaning than* mad.

Explain to students, that knowing shades of meaning of verbs and adjectives can help make their writing and speaking not only more exact, but also more interesting.

Model

Display the following chart for students. Model how to distinguish shades of meaning starting with the verbs. Help students put the words in order from slowest to fastest: *jog, run, sprint.* Guide students to think of other similar words for *run* that have different shades of meaning. (*dash, race, scamper, scurry*)

Then discuss the adjectives *hot, warm*, and *scorching.* Model how to put the words in order from least powerful to most powerful: *warm, hot, scorching.* Guide students think of other similar words for *hot* that have different shades of meaning. (*mild, steamy, stuffy, boiling*)

	Model	**Practice**
Verbs	run sprint jog	said
Adjectives	hot warm scorching	cold

Guide Practice

Tell students to brainstorm other words with similar meanings for *said* and *cold* and add their contributions to the chart. Tell students to use print or digital resources, such as a dictionary or thesaurus, to help them locate and understand the shades of meaning of the words.

Name_____ Date_____

COMMON CORE
STATE STANDARD
L.2.5b

Shades of Meaning: Verbs

Some words have almost the same **meaning**. The words **toss** and **hurl** both mean "to throw," but they have different **shades of meaning**.

I **throw** the ball to my teammate.

I **toss** the ball into the toy box. (throw gently)

I **hurl** the ball across the field. (throw hard)

Read each word pair. Write a word from the box that has almost the same meaning.

march	leap	spin	stare

1. turn, twist, _____

2. jump, hop, _____

3. walk, stroll, _____

4. peek, look, _____

COMMON CORE
STATE STANDARD
L.2.5b

Name_____ Date_____

Shades of Meaning: Verbs

Circle the word that best completes each sentence.

1. When the baby is sleeping, we have to ____.

    talk   whisper   shout

2. Our school band will ____ in the parade.

    stroll   march   walk

3. Dad told us not to ____ up and down on the bed.

    jump   hop   leap

4. I get dizzy when I ____ around in circles.

    twist   turn   spin

5. You can ____ the balloon with a pin.

    break   pop   shatter

Common Core Language Grade 2 • ©2014 Newmark Learning, LLC

COMMON CORE
STATE STANDARD
L.2.5b

Name_____ Date_____

Shades of Meaning: Adjectives

Some words have almost the same meaning. The words **slender** and **skinny** both describe things that are thin, but they have different **shades of meaning**.

A giraffe has **thin** legs that are six feet long.

Its **slender** neck is six feet long, too! (not too thin)

A baby giraffe has long, **skinny** legs. (very thin)

Read each word pair. Write a word from the box that has almost the same meaning.

cold	tiny	huge

1. big, large, _____

2. small, little, _____

3. cool, chilly, _____

Common Core
State Standard
L.2.5b

Name_____ Date_____

Shades of Meaning: Adjectives

Circle the word that <u>best</u> completes each sentence.

1. The kitten has very ____ fur.

> soft   limp   cozy

2. Don't pick the berries until they are ____ and juicy.

> heavy   plump   chubby

3. After the long race, the runners were ____.

> sleepy   bored   tired

4. The dog could not catch the ____ rabbit.

> swift   fast   rapid

5. "Please" and "thank you" are ____ words.

> nice   kind   polite

6. We all liked my sister's ____ muffins.

> good   tasty   sweet

Common Core Language Grade 2 • ©2014 Newmark Learning, LLC

Name_____ Date_____

COMMON CORE
STATE STANDARD
L.2.5b

Shades of Meaning: Verbs and Adjectives

Read each group of words. Write the words in order from weakest to strongest to show how their meanings change.

1. wet, damp, soggy

_____

_____

2. scream, cry, shout

_____

_____

3. gulp, drink, sip

_____

_____

4. dirty, grimy, dusty

_____

_____

How to Use the Practice Assessments

The quick practice assessments provided in this section are designed for easy implementation in any classroom. They can be used in several different ways. You may wish to administer a conventions assessment and a vocabulary assessment together. They may also be used individually as an informal assessment tool throughout the year. Use the following charts for item analysis and scoring.

Student Name:

Conventions	Date	Item	Standard	✔=0 X=1	Total
Assessment 1		1	**L.2.1f:** Produce, expand, and rearrange sentences.		
		2	**L.2.1c:** Use reflexive pronouns.		
		3	**L.2.2c:** Use an apostrophe to form contractions and frequently occurring possessives.		
		4	**L.2.1b:** Form and use frequently occurring irregular plural nouns.		
		5	**L.2.1e:** Use adjectives and adverbs.		
Assessment 2		1	**L.2.2a:** Capitalize holidays, product names, and geographic names.		
		2	**L.2.1b:** Form and use frequently occurring irregular plural nouns.		
		3	**L.2.2d:** Generalize spelling patterns when writing words.		
		4	**L.2.1d:** Form and use the past tense of frequently occurring irregular verbs.		
		5	**L.2.2a:** Capitalize holidays, product names, and geographic names.		
Assessment 3		1	**L.2.1f:** Produce, expand, and rearrange sentences.		
		2	**L.2.2c:** Use an apostrophe to form contractions and frequently occurring possessives.		
		3	**L.2.1b:** Form and use frequently occurring irregular plural nouns.		
		4	**L.2.2d:** Generalize spelling patterns when writing words.		
		5	**L.2.1c:** Use reflexive pronouns.		
Assessment 4		1	**L.2.2b:** Use commas in greetings and closings of letters.		
		2	**L.2.1b:** Form and use frequently occurring irregular plural nouns.		
		3	**L.2.1d:** Form and use the past tense of frequently occurring irregular verbs.		
		4	**L.2.1f:** Produce, expand, and rearrange sentences.		

Student Name:

Vocabulary	Date	Item	Standard	✔=0 X=1	Total
Assessment 1		1	**L.2.4e:** Use glossaries and dictionaries, both print and digital, to determine or clarify the meaning of words and phrases.		
		2	**L.2.4e:** Use glossaries and dictionaries, both print and digital, to determine or clarify the meaning of words and phrases.		
		3	**L.2.4e:** Use glossaries and dictionaries, both print and digital, to determine or clarify the meaning of words and phrases.		
		4	**L.2.4a:** Use sentence-level context as a clue to the meaning of a word or phrase.		
Assessment 2		1	**L.2.4d:** Use knowledge of the meaning of individual words to predict the meaning of compound words.		
		2	**L.2.4a:** Use sentence-level context as a clue to the meaning of a word or phrase.		
		3	**L.2.4c:** Use a known root word as a clue to the meaning of an unknown word with the same root.		
		4	**L.2.5a:** Identify real-life connections between words and their use.		
Assessment 3		1	**L.2.4a:** Use sentence-level context as a clue to the meaning of a word or phrase.		
		2	**L.2.4d:** Use knowledge of the meaning of individual words to predict the meaning of compound words.		
		3	**L.2.4c:** Use a known root word as a clue to the meaning of an unknown word with the same root.		
		4	**L.2.5a:** Identify real-life connections between words and their use.		
Assessment 4		1	**L.2.4a:** Use sentence-level context as a clue to the meaning of a word or phrase.		
		2	**L.2.5a:** Identify real-life connections between words and their use.		
		3	**L.2.6:** Use words and phrases acquired through conversations, reading and being read to, and responding to texts.		
		4	**L.2.4b:** Determine the meaning of the new word formed when a known prefix is added to a known word.		

Name_____ Date_____

Read the passage. Choose the answer that best corrects each underlined part.

How Animals Move

Animals move in many different ways. [1] <u>They may jump. They may fly. They may walk. They may swim.</u> They have different body parts that help them move. Frogs have strong legs for jumping. [2] <u>They use their legs to push ourselves up.</u> Birds have wings for flying. [3] <u>The bones in a bird's wings are very light.</u> This makes flying easier. [4] <u>Ducks have foots with webbed, or connected, toes.</u> [5] <u>This body part lets them move through the water quick.</u>

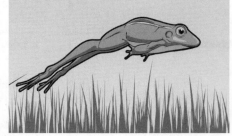

1. Ⓐ They may jump. They may fly walk swim.
   Ⓑ They may jump, fly, walk, or swim.
   Ⓒ They may jump. Fly, walk, swim.
   Ⓓ No change.

Common Core Language Grade 2 • ©2014 Newmark Learning, LLC

Name_____ Date_____

2. Ⓐ They use their legs to push herself up.

Ⓑ They use their legs to push myself up.

Ⓒ They use their legs to push themselves up.

Ⓓ No change.

3. Ⓐ The bones in a birds' wings are very light.

Ⓑ The bone's in a bird's wings are very light.

Ⓒ The bones in a birds wings are very light.

Ⓓ No change.

4. Ⓐ Ducks have footses with webbed, or connected, toes.

Ⓑ Ducks have feets with webbed, or connected, toes.

Ⓒ Ducks have feet with webbed, or connected, toes.

Ⓓ No change.

5. Ⓐ This body part lets them move quick through the water.

Ⓑ This body part lets them move quickly through the water.

Ⓒ This body part lets them quick move through the water.

Ⓓ No change.

Common Core
State Standards

L.2.1–
L.2.3

Name_____ Date_____

Read the passage. Choose the answer that best corrects each underlined part.

Jin's First Day

Jin pushed pieces of cereal around in his bowl of milk. [1] <u>Maybe if he never finished his Fun flakes</u>, he would never have to leave the house.

"Okay," his mom said. [2] <u>"It's time to brush your teeths and get ready to go."</u> She took Jin's bowl and put it in the sink.

"I don't know, Mom," Jin said. "My head hurts. I don't think I should go to school."

[3] <u>"It's going to be fin,"</u> his mom said. "I promise."

But Jin wasn't so sure. Today was his first day at a new school.

[4] <u>At his old school in Texas, he knowed everyone.</u>

[5] <u>At his new school in ohio, he didn't know a single kid.</u>

Common Core Language Grade 2 • ©2014 Newmark Learning, LLC

COMMON CORE
STATE STANDARDS
L.2.1–
L.2.3

Name_____ Date_____

1. Ⓐ Maybe if he never finished his fun flakes
   Ⓑ Maybe if he never finished his Fun Flakes
   Ⓒ Maybe if he never finished his fun Flakes
   Ⓓ No change.

2. Ⓐ "It's time to brush your tooths and get ready to go."
   Ⓑ "It's time to brush your tooth and get ready to go."
   Ⓒ "It's time to brush your teeth and get ready to go."
   Ⓓ No change.

3. Ⓐ "Its going to be fin,"
   Ⓑ "It's going to be fine,"
   Ⓒ "It's not going to be fin,"
   Ⓓ No change.

4. Ⓐ At his old school in Texas. He knowed everyone.
   Ⓑ At his old school in texas, he knowed everyone.
   Ⓒ At his old school in Texas, he knew everyone.
   Ⓓ No change.

5. Ⓐ At his new school in ohio. He didn't know a single kid.
   Ⓑ At his new school in Ohio, he didn't know a single kid.
   Ⓒ At his new school in ohio, he didn't knew a single kid.
   Ⓓ No change.

COMMON CORE
STATE STANDARDS

L.2.1–
L.2.3

Name_____ Date_____

Read the passage. Choose the answer that best corrects each underlined part.

Venus Flytraps

You may know that insects eat plants. But did you know that there is a plant that eats insects? [1] Flies, spiders, and other insects are eaten by a Venus flytrap. This plant has a special way of catching and eating its food. [2] It has pairs of leaves that open and close like a clams shell. [3] The leaves have a sweetly juice on them that insects want. [4] When an insect comes for the juice, the two leaves snap shut. The insect is trapped. [5] It can not free myself.

1. Ⓐ Flies, spiders, and other insects. Are eaten by a Venus flytrap.

   Ⓑ Flies are eaten by a Venus flytrap. Spiders are eaten by a Venus flytrap. Other insects are eaten by a Venus flytrap.

   Ⓒ A Venus flytrap eats flies, spiders, and other insects.

   Ⓓ No change.

COMMON CORE STATE STANDARDS

L.2.1– L.2.3

Name_____ Date_____

2. Ⓐ It has pairs of leaves that open and close like a clam's shell.

    Ⓑ It has pairs of leaves that open and close. Like a clams shell.

    Ⓒ It has pairs of leaves that open and close like a clams' shell.

    Ⓓ No change.

3. Ⓐ The leaves have a sweetily juice on them that insects want.

    Ⓑ The leaves have a sweet juice on them that insects want.

    Ⓒ The leaves have a sweetly juicy on them that insects want.

    Ⓓ No change.

4. Ⓐ When an insect comes for the juice, the leaves snap chut.

    Ⓑ When an insect comes for the juice, the leaves snap shute.

    Ⓒ When an insect comes for the juice, the leafs snap chut.

    Ⓓ No change.

5. Ⓐ It can not free themselves.

    Ⓑ It can not free itself.

    Ⓒ It can not free herself.

    Ⓓ No change.

COMMON CORE
STATE STANDARDS
L.2.1–
L.2.3

Name_____ Date_____

Rewrite the letter below. Fix the spelling, punctuation, and grammar mistakes in the underlined sentences, or just rewrite them in a better way.

[1] <u>Dear Shelby</u>

I am writing to you from Vermont. My family is staying in a cabin by a lake. [2] <u>Yesterday, we saw a bunch of fishes swimming there!</u> [3] <u>We have spended lots of time outside.</u> [4] <u>Today, a mountain was climbed by us and sandwiches were eaten by us.</u>

Write back soon!

Your friend,

Manuel

Name_____ Date_____

_____

_____

_____

_____

_____

_____

_____

_____

_____

COMMON CORE
STATE STANDARDS
L.2.4–
L.2.6

Name_____ Date_____

Read the dictionary entries for the words below. Use them to answer the questions.

brilliant (BRIL-yunt)

adjective

1. very shiny or bright

2. very smart

notice (NOH-tis)

noun

1. a warning or piece of news

verb

2. to see or observe

pen (PEN)

noun

1. a tool for writing or drawing in ink

2. a closed or fenced-in place to keep animals

sink (SINK)

verb

1. to fall slowly to a lower place

noun

2. a bowl connected to a water source

Common Core Language Grade 2 • ©2014 Newmark Learning, LLC

Name_____ Date_____

1. Which two words may be used as a verb or a noun?
   Ⓐ brilliant and sink
   Ⓑ pen and brilliant
   Ⓒ notice and sink
   Ⓓ pen and sink

2. Which of these is a meaning for the word **pen**?
   Ⓐ a closed or fenced-in place to keep animals
   Ⓑ very shiny or bright
   Ⓒ to fall slowly to a lower place
   Ⓓ to see or observe

3. Which of these words is an adjective?
   Ⓐ pen
   Ⓑ notice
   Ⓒ sink
   Ⓓ brilliant

4. Which of these sentences uses the word **sink** as a verb?
   Ⓐ I washed my hands in the sink.
   Ⓑ I filled the sink with water.
   Ⓒ The sink is full of dirty dishes.
   Ⓓ I watched the rock sink into the pond.

Name_____ Date_____

Read the passage below. Then answer the questions.

Hummingbirds

Hummingbirds are some of the smallest birds on Earth. Their wings flap so quickly that they are hard to see. The wings make a humming sound as they flap.

Hummingbirds feed on flowers. They hover, or hang in the air, by the flowers. They use their long beaks to pull out nectar, or sweet juice. In the winter, hummingbirds fly to warm places to find flowers. They may also eat small insects for food.

There are many kinds of hummingbirds. They live all over North and South America. Ruby-throated hummingbirds live in North and Central America. They are named for their ruby, or red, throats. These colorful birds lay tiny eggs. Each egg is the size of a pea!

Name_____ Date_____

1. Which of these tells what the compound word **hummingbird** means?

   Ⓐ bird that hangs in the air

   Ⓑ bird that flies

   Ⓒ bird that hums

   Ⓓ bird with small wings

2. What do you think the word **hover** means?

   Ⓐ feed on flowers

   Ⓑ red

   Ⓒ sweet juice

   Ⓓ hang in the air

3. Which of these tells the meaning of the word **colorful**?

   Ⓐ without color

   Ⓑ full of color

   Ⓒ someone who colors

   Ⓓ relating to color

4. The passage uses the words **tiny** and **small**. Which of the words below has almost the same meaning?

   Ⓐ big

   Ⓑ red

   Ⓒ little

   Ⓓ fast

COMMON CORE
STATE STANDARDS
L.2.4–
L.2.6

Name_____ Date_____

Read the passage below. Then answer the questions.

Ellie's Broken Leg

Ellie didn't just break her leg. She broke it at the worst time ever. Every year, her class spent the last week of school having a Fitness Fun Fair. All week, they played games like kickball and frog jump. During kickball, Ellie sat with her broken leg in a cast. She cheered for her team, but she felt cheerless. It was painful to not play.

The last day of the Fitness Fun Fair was sack race day. She walked from the car to the school feeling sadder with each step. But when she got to the schoolyard, she didn't see a sack race. She saw her class sitting at a table full of art tools. There were markers, glue, and tape. There were fuzzy pom-poms.

"We have a change of plans," said Ellie's teacher. "Today is Decorate Ellie's Cast Day!"

Soon Ellie's cast was full of pom-poms and drawings. She felt a lot better about wearing it.

Common Core Language Grade 2 • ©2014 Newmark Learning, LLC

Name_____ Date_____

1. Which of these words are clues to the meaning of the word **cast**?

    Ⓐ broken leg

    Ⓑ kickball

    Ⓒ favorite

    Ⓓ fuzzy

2. Which of these words are compound words?

    Ⓐ sports, games

    Ⓑ glue, markers

    Ⓒ sadder, teacher

    Ⓓ kickball, schoolyard

3. Which of these words has a suffix that means "a person who"?

    Ⓐ cheerless

    Ⓑ teacher

    Ⓒ painful

    Ⓓ fitness

4. The class uses fuzzy pom-poms to decorate Ellie's cast. Which of the things below is also fuzzy?

    Ⓐ a stuffed animal

    Ⓑ a fork

    Ⓒ a wooden desk

    Ⓓ a piece of paper

COMMON CORE
STATE STANDARDS
L.2.4–
L.2.6

Name_____ Date_____

Read the passage below. Then answer the questions.

City to Country

People live in different places. Life is different in every place.

An urban area is a big city where many people live. The buildings are very close together there. Most people live in apartments, or small parts of big buildings. They walk or take trains and buses to get around. Urban areas may be loud and crowded.

A suburban area is a less crowded place that is still close to a city. There is more space between buildings. Many people live in houses. They use cars to get around. Stores are grouped together in shopping centers or malls.

A rural area is a place with few buildings. It has lots of open land. This land may be used for farming or raising animals. Homes in rural areas are far apart. This place is perfect for people who want a quiet and unrushed life.

COMMON CORE
STATE STANDARDS
L.2.4–
L.2.6

Name_____ Date_____

1. Which of these words are clues to the meaning of the word **urban**?

   Ⓐ big city

   Ⓑ less crowded

   Ⓒ far apart

   Ⓓ raising animals

2. Which of these words name different kinds of homes?

   Ⓐ crowded, space

   Ⓑ house, apartment

   Ⓒ farming, raising

   Ⓓ eat, shop

3. Which of these words describes a rural area?

   Ⓐ crowded

   Ⓑ loud

   Ⓒ city

   Ⓓ quiet

4. Which of these tells the meaning of **unrushed**?

   Ⓐ rushed again

   Ⓑ very rushed

   Ⓒ not rushed

   Ⓓ rushed before

Answer Key, pages 7–15

page 7

1. c
2. f
3. e
4. a
5. b
6. d

page 9

1. a <u>den</u> of snakes
2. a <u>prickle</u> of hedgehogs
3. a <u>streak</u> of tigers
4. a <u>mob</u> of emus
5. a <u>charm</u> of hummingbirds
6. a <u>trip</u> of sheep
7. a <u>horde</u> of hamsters
8. a <u>knot</u> of frogs
9. a <u>bed</u> of clams
10. a <u>leap</u> of leopards

L	E	A	P	D	E	N
C	M	T	R	I	P	L
H	X	Z	I	W	P	H
A	R	K	B	C	H	J	O
R	N	D	K	Y	M	R
M	O	B	L	P	O	D
S	T	R	E	A	K	E

page 8

1. flight
2. bouquet
3. pair
4. crowd

page 11

1. c
2. a
3. b

page 13

1. geese
2. sheep
3. women
4. people

page 14

1. mice
2. feet
3. children
4. women
5. men
6. people

page 15

(sample answers shown)

1. *The two men went to the store.*
2. *There are five people at the party.*
3. *All the fish swam together.*
4. *I brush my teeth before I go to sleep.*

page 12

1. men
2. fish
3. mice
4. feet
5. teeth
6. children

Answer Key, pages 17-25

page 17

1. She built a toy car all by (herself.)
2. They bought (themselves) a basketball.
3. I taught (myself) how to play piano.
4. Tim walked home from school by (himself.)
5. We clean our room (ourselves.)

page 18

1. myself
2. himself
3. itself
4. yourselves
5. ourselves

page 19

1. We painted the room (ourselves.)
   Sample: We made ourselves a snack.
2. I fell on the sidewalk and hurt (myself.)
   Sample: I bought myself a new shirt.
3. Make (yourselves) comfortable.
   Sample: Help yourselves to lunch.

page 21

1. hid
2. took
3. told
4. sat
5. read
6. ate

page 22

1. bit
2. knew
3. kept
4. cut
5. flew
6. bought

page 23

						¹F	E	L	L		²H	A	³D
⁴F	O	⁵R	G	A	V	E					E		U
	O		O			L			⁶R	A	N	G
⁷U	N	D	E	R	⁸S	T	O	O	⁹D		R	
G		E			A				R		¹⁰D	I	¹¹D
H			¹²L	I	T				A				R
¹³T	O	L	D		D		¹⁴W	E	N	T			E
					K								W

page 24

1. found
2. paid
3. held
4. met

page 25

(sample answers shown)

1. We sang a song.
2. They came to watch the game.
3. We won the contest.

Answer Key, pages 27-33

page 27

1. My <u>blanket</u> is (soft.)
2. I love to eat (spicy) food.
3. The <u>elephants</u> are (huge.)
4. Take out this (smelly) garbage.

page 28

1. The **heavy** box was hard to lift.
2. Pretzels are a **salty** snack.
3. The wet floor is very **slippery**.
4. We have **pink** roses in our garden.
5. The birds were so **noisy**, they woke me up.
6. *Sample answers: My pink shirt is my favorite. The noisy dog barked at the squirrel.*

page 29

1. The girls <u>swing</u> (high) in the air.
2. Sam (quickly) <u>climbs</u> the rock wall.
3. I <u>eat</u> (downstairs) in the kitchen.
4. The <u>children</u> <u>went</u> to the park (yesterday.)
5. The boys <u>walked</u> (slowly) to school.
6. We <u>swam</u> in the pool (today.)

page 30

1. The turtle moves **slowly** across the grass.
2. I **usually** go to bed at eight o'clock.
3. Please carry the glass vase **carefully**.
4. The boys came **inside** because it was raining.
5. It is noon, so we will eat lunch **soon**.
6. *Sample answer: <u>Usually</u> I walk home <u>slowly</u>.*

page 31

1. The (happy) baby smiles at her mom.
(adjective)
The baby gurgles (happily.)
(adverb)
2. Our music teacher sings (beautifully.)
(adverb)
"America" is a (beautiful) song.
(adjective)

page 32

1. The runner **quickly** sprints around the track.

   The **quick** runner crosses the finish line.
2. We heard a **loud** boom of thunder.

   Thunder crashes **loudly** during the storm.
3. Kim was **sleepy** at the end of the night.

   She yawned **sleepily** as she went to bed.
4. The ballet dancer moves **gracefully**.

   The star of the show is a **graceful** dancer.
5. Your speech was **clear**.

   You spoke **clearly** during your speech.

page 33

(sample answers shown)

1. *I spoke in a **quiet** voice.*
   *I spoke **quietly**.*
2. *I am **careful** with the glass vase.*
   *I hold the glass vase **carefully**.*
3. *There is a **slow** car in front of us.*
   *I move **slowly** when I am tired.*

Answer Key, pages 35-43

page 35

1. No

2. Yes

3. No

page 36 (sample answers shown)

1. My grandma *has a garden.*

2. *Pandas* live in the zoo.

3. The bus driver *picked up the kids.*

4. *We* won the game!

5. *My birthday party* was fun.

6. *The kittens* are so small.

page 37

(sample answers shown)

1. The tall giraffe eats leaves from the tree.

2. What sport does your older brother play?

3. I held a huge snake at the science museum!

page 38

(sample answers shown)

1. *Emma wears a **bright** scarf.*

2. *Look at that **huge** bug **on the wall**!*

3. *Our class is taking a trip **to a farm**.*

4. *Did you see the **funny animal** show?*

5. *Rico went to the **sunny** beach **to go swimming**.*

page 39

1. The babysitter watched the twins.

2. Lin painted a picture of the sunrise.

3. Joe solved the problem!

4. The zoo animals made the escape.

page 40

1. The hikers climbed the mountain.

2. Our class read this book.

3. Raj bought a new car.

4. My dog chased the truck.

5. Mom planted these flowers.

page 41

1. Leo likes strawberries, **but** he does not like blueberries.

2. Should we go to the store now, **or** should we go after dinner?

3. They went to the movies, **and** then they went to the store.

page 42

1. Sasha went to sleep, ***but*** Marta stayed up late.

2. I washed the dishes, ***and*** I took out the garbage.

3. The boys went fishing, ***but*** they did not catch any fish.

4. Do you want juice, ***or*** do you want milk?

page 43

1. Tomas has a **new** game, and we played it **together**.

2. The children talk **quietly** inside, but they yell **loudly** outside.

3. Do you want **iced** tea, or do you want **hot** coffee?

Answer Key, pages 44-51

page 44

(sample answers shown)

1. Mia runs *quickly*, but her little sister walks *slowly*.

2. Pick up that *small* chair, and move it over there *against the wall*.

3. Is this your *brown* bag, or is that *red* bag yours?

4. Lee pets the *soft* cat, and the cat purrs *loudly*.

page 45

1. *Kelly brought the food, and Sal brought the drinks.*

2. *Manny passed the ball, and Dax caught it.*

3. *The girls watched a funny movie, but the boys watched a scary movie.*

page 46

(sample answers shown)

1. *The boy colored a picture, and his mom hung it up.*

2. *Grandpa baked the muffins, and Aunt Liz cooked the eggs.*

3. *Eva won a blue ribbon, but her cat ripped it.*

4. *Paulo played the drums, and his brother played the guitar.*

page 47

(sample answers shown)

1. *California is sunny.*

2. *It has many mountains.*

3. *California is sunny, and it has many mountains.*

4. *California is warm and sunny, and it has many tall mountains.*

page 49

1. Memorial Day

2. Columbus Day

3. Mother's Day

4. New Year's Day

page 50

1. We went to my grandma's house for Thanksgiving.

2. My first day of school is after Labor Day.

3. We made a Father's Day card for our dad.

4. I do not have school on Presidents' Day.

5. A soldier talked to our class on Veterans Day.

page 51

1. Tommy's Tricycles

2. Grumpy's Granola

3. Grassy Farms Yogurt

4. Giant Grin Toothpaste

Answer Key, pages 52-61

page 52

1. My puppy loves Begging Bulldog Biscuits.

2. Dad cooked dinner with Italy's Best Pasta.

3. We bought a pack of Bright Night Lightbulbs.

4. Answers will vary, but product name should be capitalized

page 53

1. Empire State Building

2. Texas

3. Mississippi River

4. Rocky Mountains

page 54

1. We took a trip to the Grand Canyon.

2. I live on a street called Pine Lane.

3. Ada went swimming in Lake Michigan.

4. My cousin lives in Chicago.

5. *Sample Answer: My family took a vacation to Seattle, Washington.*

page 55

2. We paddled a canoe on Lake Washington.

3. My favorite cereal is Crunchy Oat Flakes.

4. Answers will vary, but holiday should be capitalized

page 57

Correct: 1, 3, 4

page 58

1. Correct

2. Hi Aisha,

3. Hello Dad,

4. Greetings friends,

page 59

Correct: 1, 6

page 60

1. friend,

2. Correct

3. Regards,

4. Thanks,

5. Correct

6. Love,

7. Best wishes,

8. Best,

9. Correct

10. Thank you,

page 61

(sample answers shown)

1. May 12, 2015
   Dear Grandma,
   My new puppy is here. Come visit us soon!
   Love,
   Olivia

2. November 5, 2015
   Hi Uncle John,
   We can't wait to see you at Thanksgiving.
   Sincerely,
   Jack

Answer Key, pages 63–71

page 63

1. b
2. d
3. e
4. c
5. a

page 64

1. **It's** your turn to do the dishes.
2. **You'd** better give my hat back.
3. I **didn't** take your hat!
4. **I'm** leaving for school now.
5. **We'll** pick you up.
6. **They're** on the soccer team.
7. **She's** really good at math.
8. I **couldn't** eat another bite.

page 65

1. the games Tom owns

   (Tom's games)

2. the toys the girls have

   (the girls' toys)

3. the shirts the men have

   (the men's shirts)

4. the pets the kids own

   (the kids' pets)

page 66

1. Gwen's apple is red.
2. The women's car needs to be fixed.
3. The parents' rules were tough.
4. The people's houses will be sold today.

page 67

1. Ben's
2. can't
3. friend's
4. grandparents'
5. cat's
6. They'll

page 69

1. toy, coin
2. page, bridge

page 70

1. tape
2. kite
3. tub
4. fin
5. cane

page 71

1. sh
2. sh
3. ch
4. sh
5. ch
6. ch

Answer Key, pages 73–85

page 73

1. eyesight
2. lax
3. (palace)
4. remove

page 75

1. formal
2. informal
3. formal
4. informal

page 76

(sample answers shown)

1. I like your shoes very much.
2. We enjoyed ourselves at the zoo.
3. Can't wait to see you guys tomorrow!

page 79

1. large
2. messy
3. rip

page 80

(sample answers shown)

1. hit something and come back up
2. huge; very large
3. sit on top of water or other liquid
4. writer
5. catch

page 81

1. quiet way of talking (underline: talk; don't wake up)
2. funny (underline: laughing)
3. dirt (underline: plant the seeds)
4. windy (underline: blew back and forth)

page 83

1. (re)think: to think again
2. (un)fair: not fair
3. (re)view: to view again
4. (un)true: not true
5. (re)read: to read again
6. (un)clear: not clear

page 84

1. misspell; c
2. preheat; e
3. repack; a
4. unkind; f
5. miscount; b
6. pretest; d

page 85

1. repaint; paint again
2. misbehave; behave badly
3. unfair; not fair
4. preview; watch before
5. unlucky; not lucky
6. remake; make again

Answer Key, pages 87-93

page 87

1. e
2. f
3. d
4. b
5. c
6. a

page 88

1. Circle: sad
   Underline: -ness
   Write: sad
2. Circle: color
   Underline: -ful
   Write: color
3. Circle: care
   Underline: -less
   Write: care
4. Circle: play
   Underline: -er
   Write: plays
5. Circle: help
   Underline: -less
   Write: help
6. Circle: cheer
   Underline: -ful
   Write: cheer
7. Circle: farm
   Underline: -er
   Write: farms

page 89

(sample answers shown)

1. full of help; giving help
2. one who teaches
3. state of being ill or sick
4. relating to a certain season
5. without wires

page 91

1. skateboard
2. toothbrush
3. starfish
4. sidewalk
5. firefly

page 92

1. **outside**
   out, side
2. **pancakes**
   pan, cakes
3. **blueberry**
   blue, berry
4. **footprints**
   foot, prints
5. **backpacks**
   back, packs
6. **rainbow**
   rain, bow

page 93

1. backpack
2. basketball
3. raincoat
4. sunglasses

Answer Key, pages 95–107

page 95
1. egg
2. larva
3. pupa
4. adult

page 96
1. c
2. a
3. d
4. b

page 97
(sample answers shown)
1. a long, deep cut
2. great happiness
3. force your way in
4. movement

page 99
1. juicy
2. stinky
3. spicy
4. smoky

page 100
1. sweet
2. fresh
3. tasty
4. fragrant

page 101
1. palace
2. cabin
3. den
4. apartment
5. hive

page 103
1. spin
2. leap
3. march
4. stare

page 104
1. whisper
2. march
3. jump
4. spin
5. pop

page 105
1. huge
2. tiny
3. cold

page 106
1. soft
2. plump
3. tired
4. swift
5. polite
6. tasty

Answer Key, pages 110–127

page 107

(sample answers shown)

1. damp, wet, soggy

2. cry, shout, scream

3. sip, drink, gulp

4. dusty, dirty, grimy

pages 110–111

1. b

2. c

3. d

4. c

5. b

page 113

1. b

2. c

3. b

4. c

5. b

pages 114–115

1. c

2. a

3. b

4. d

5. b

page 117

(sample answers shown)

1. Dear Shelby,

2. Yesterday we saw a bunch of fish swimming there.

3. We have spent lots of time outside.

4. Today we climbed a mountain and ate sandwiches.

page 119

1. c

2. a

3. d

4. d

page 121

1. c

2. d

3. b

4. c

page 123

1. a

2. d

3. b

4. a

page 125

1. a

2. b

3. d

4. c

Common Core Language Grade 2 • ©2014 Newmark Learning, LLC